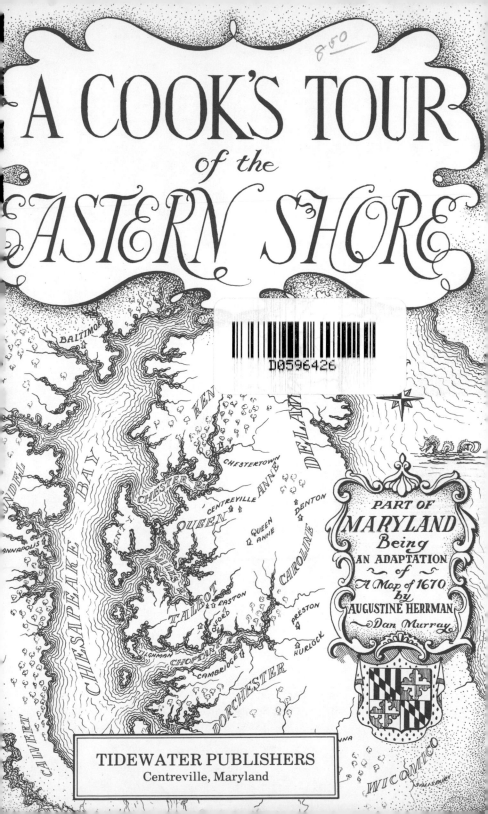

# A COOK'S TOUR
## of the
# EASTERN SHORE

PART OF
MARYLAND
Being
AN ADAPTATION
of
A Map of 1670
by
AUGUSTINE HERRMAN
Dan Murray

TIDEWATER PUBLISHERS
Centreville, Maryland

Walk up the boxwood path and through the open door. We welcome you to our book.

In it are gathered the favorite recipes from the friends and members of

## THE JUNIOR AUXILIARY.

And through it we hope to win new friends for

## THE MEMORIAL HOSPITAL
### at
## EASTON, MARYLAND

## COMPILED, EDITED AND DECORATED BY
## THE COOK BOOK COMMITTEE

Mrs. Howard Bloomfield, Editor
Mrs. Charles E. Wheeler, Assistant Editor
Mrs. Howard Kinnamon, Advertising Manager
Mrs. Frank Gunther, Circulation
Mrs. Frank Gregson, Publicity
Mrs. Paul Detrich, Business Manager

Mrs. John Swaine, Jr., Chairman
Mrs. Thomas Cover, Jr., Mrs. Douglas Hanks,
Mrs. Harvey Jarboe, Mrs. Davis Kirby, Jr.,
Mrs. Howe Lagarde, Mrs. Harry Rossiter,
Mrs. Dale Elrich, Mrs. Kurt Lederer,
Mrs. C. P. Merrick, Jr., Mrs. Ronald Nevins,
Mrs. Earl Todd

### ARTISTS

The Cover -- Mr. John B. Moll, Jr.
The Map -- Mr. Daniel Murray
The Foreword -- Mrs. A. C. Dodge
The Dividers -- Mrs. Howard Staley
Sketches -- Mrs. W. T. Hammond, Miss Susan
Norton-Taylor, Mrs. Charles E. Wheeler,
Mrs. John Noble, Miss Elizabeth Booraem,
Mr. Frank Gregson, Mrs. Nelson Jeffress,
Mrs. William E. Shannahan, Tom French-Norton

### PENMEN

Mrs. John Noble, Miss Barbara Bromfield
Mrs. William Lane, Mrs. Thomson Firth, Jr.,
Mrs. Charles E. Wheeler, Mrs. Robert F.
Soderberg, Mrs. Ernest Heinmuller, Anne B.
Perry, Mrs. James T. Ferguson

# CONTENTS

# PUNCH BOWL

# BLOSSOM COCKTAIL

1 ounce Grenadine
2 ounces lemon juice
1 cup unsweetened pineapple juice
1 small egg white

Put all ingredients in cocktail shaker with crushed ice and shake vigorously. Serve at once in cocktail glasses with or without a cherry and small wedge of pineapple.

Mrs. Raymond O. Dean

## TEA PUNCH

1 pint Jamaica Rum
1 pint Sherry Wine
1 pint strong green tea
½ pint whiskey
1 orange          1 lemon

Combine ingredients and let punch stand several hours before serving.

Mrs. Samuel T. Kennard

# PINEAPPLE TEA

2 quarts tea
juice of 6 lemons
3 quarts gingerale
1 can crushed pineapple
3 cups sugar or sugar syrup

Mix all ingredients and chill.

Mrs. Raymond O. Dean

# SAUTERNE PUNCH

2 gallons orange and lemon juice
6 bottles sauterne
1 bottle cognac
1 bottle sugar syrup
½ gallon lime ice
6 bottles sparkling water

Mix all ingredients except sparkling water. Pour this in very slowly as punch is being served.

Serves 50.

Mrs. Frank Gregson

## APPOLINARIS TEA

2 quarts strong tea          3 oranges
5 cups sugar                 12 lemons
    1 bottle maraschino cherries
    1 can pineapple chunks
    2 quarts Appolinaris

Squeeze oranges and lemons, and pour hot tea over rinds and allow to stand a few minutes. Strain, add sugar, and when cool add other ingredients. Open Appolinaris only when ready to serve.

Mrs. B. C. Voshell

## FRUIT PUNCH

12 lemons                18 oranges
4 cups sugar             4 cups water
    1 quart gingerale
1 quart gin   or  2 quarts gingerale

Squeeze lemons and oranges. Boil sugar and water together. Grate rind of fruit and add to syrup. Add other ingredients, ice and serve.

S. Wayman Delahay

# PARTY PUNCH

1 large can pineapple juice
1 large can orange juice
5 lemons          2/3 cup sugar
1½ quarts gingerale

Mix all together and pour over ice.

Mrs. John Swaine

# SPICED TEA

4 tablespoons black tea
2 tablespoons whole cloves
½ cup strained lemon juice
1 cup strained orange juice
½ cup sugar - or more
2 quarts boiling water

Pour 1 quart boiling water over tea
and cloves and let steep 5 minutes.
Strain and add fruit juices and the
sugar. Stir until dissolved, add the
other quart of boiling water. Serve
very hot.

Mrs. Jerome Frampton, Jr.

# MINT PUNCH

4 large bunches mint
juice of 6 lemons
juice of 6 oranges
juice of 4 grapefruit
1 quart of pineapple juice
2 pounds sugar
4 quarts water

Pinch leaves from mint stalks and crush thoroughly. Pour lemon juice over mint and let stand 1 hour. Make syrup of sugar and water and pour over lemon and mint. Cool and strain. Add remaining juices, chill and serve.

Mrs. Thomas Carpenter

# GEORGIE'S TEA PUNCH

1 quart strong tea
1 quart red wine
6 lemons
2 pounds sugar — 1 pint water

Squeeze lemons and pour the pint of boiling water over the cut rinds. Strain and boil this water with the sugar. Cool syrup, mix with other ingredients and pour over crushed ice.

Mrs. William H. Norris

## EGGNOG OTWELL

Beat the yolks of 12 eggs and the whites of 2 until as light as possible.

Add a level tablespoon of powdered sugar for each egg, and beat into the yolks.

Pour slowly into the above, 1 pint of brandy, 2 pints whiskey, ½ pint of rum; stirring rapidly as you add the liquor.

When well mixed, add 3 pints of milk and 4 pints of cream. No liquor must be added after the cream and milk.

Mrs. S. N. Hersloff

## EGG NOG

| 10 eggs | 1 pound of sugar — or less |
|---|---|
| 1 fifth of whiskey | 1 cup of rum |
| 1 quart of cream | 2 quarts rich milk |

Beat the egg yolks, adding the sugar slowly. Pour in the whiskey very gradually. Then add the rum.

Stir in the milk, then the cream. Fold in the stiffly beaten egg whites.

Mrs. Samuel W. Bratt

# SHERRY COBBLER

1 heaping teaspoon sugar (less if you
    haven't a sweet tooth)
1 dash of lime juice
1 curl of lime rind
2 ounces sherry
Cracked ice

Mix sugar, lime juice and rind with
a bit of water to help melt sugar, in
highball glass. Add sherry and fill
glass to top with cracked ice. Stir
and serve.

Mrs. Howe Lagarde

# HORS D'ŒUVRES & CANAPÉS

Stuffed olives wrapped in bacon and broiled.

Frankfurters, inch pieces, in pastry or biscuit dough, and baked

Pastry turnovers with mincemeat, jam, or cheese.

Chicken livers, wrapped in bacon and broiled.

Butter creamed with parsley, onion and lemon juice topped with caviar or egg.

Anchovies on small triangles of toast, spread with lemon butter.

Small rounds of bread, with cucumber, then fine slice of onion - paprika.

Mince capers with butter, spread on circles of bread.

Shredded tuna fish mixed with lemon juice and mayonnaise.

Sardine paste mixed with lemon juice salt and Worcestershire.

Deviled ham mixed with chopped hard cooked egg and horseradish.

# CHEESE PUFFS

½ pound cheddar cheese ,grated
½ cup butter
1 cup flour
dash cayenne

Blend cheese and butter, add flour and cayenne. Chill in the refrigerator for 2 or 3 hours.

Roll into balls 1 inch in diameter.

Bake in a hot oven 450° for 15 minutes.

Mrs. Thomas M. Carpenter

# CHEESE SNACKS

1 pound margarine
1 pound sharp American cheese—grated
½ - ¾ can paprika
1½ pounds flour

Mix all ingredients thoroughly. Chill for 24 hours. Let dough thaw or work again until pliable enough to put through cookie press or meat grinder. Cut in bite size pieces and bake in 450° oven until brown. These will keep well in air tight can.

Mrs. Albert Holland

# Cheese Roll

1/2 pound Raquefort cheese
2 packages Old English Cheese
2 packages Philadelphia Cream Cheese
1 teaspoon mustard (Bohemian)
Dash of tabasco
1 onion (small) grated

Mix above ingredients until smooth. Use mix master if available. Place in ice box over night. In the morning form in a mold and place back in ice box until ready to serve. Roll mold in ground nuts before serving.

Mrs. Howard F. Kinnamon

# PARISIAN SPREAD

1 quart tomatoes
1 pound chipped beef
1 pound sharp cheese
¼ pound butter
Salt, pepper, cayenne to taste
1 egg

Cook tomatoes until reduced to 1 cup. Put chipped beef and cheese through meat grinder and add to the tomato. Cook until well blended. Add butter and seasonings. Take from fire and stir in slightly beaten egg. Store in refrigerator. May be used as sandwich spread, hot or cold; and as a canapé spread.

Wye Town Farm

# CHEESE DROPS

Beat 1 egg until light, add 1 cup grated cheese, bread crumbs and mix well. Season with 1 teaspoon Sherry and 1 teaspoon catsup and dash of paprika. Wet the hands and form balls size of a cherry, dip in egg, then in crumbs and fry in hot fat until light brown. Serve hot.

Mrs. Howard Hill

# JELLIED EGGS

These are tasty and attractive as hors d'oeuvres, although they may be served as a first course.

Make some beef broth or consommé that will jell firmly. Cook eggs about 4 minutes. They should not be hard - but the whites must be firm enough to permit perfect shelling.

Put broth in a deep pan or ramekins when cool. Arrange eggs so that each will be an island in a sea of jelly. The eggs should be stripped with fresh tarragon - or pimiento or mint leaves can be used to look decorative and add flavor. Tuck parsley all around the dish and chill until firm.

Jack Gill

# CANAPE SPREAD

1 package Velveeta cheese melted in ¼ cup milk. Remove from stove and add 1 teaspoon chopped onion, 1 small can pimientoes chopped, salt and dash red pepper. Cool and store in refrigerator.

Mrs. Jennings B. Quillin

# WINDRUSH CANAPE SPREAD

1 package cream cheese
1 onion, grated
cream
Worcestershire sauce
mustard

Soften the cheese and add cream until the consistency of whipped cream. Add a dash of Worcestershire sauce, and a dash of mustard to taste.

Serve with potato chips to be used as dunkers.

Mrs. Grace Wilford

## CREAM CHEESE SPREAD OR STUFFING

3 cakes cream cheese
1/2 cup chopped pecans
1/2 cup chopped sweet pickles
1/2 cup chopped stuffed olives
1/2 cup chopped celery

Soften cheese with mayonnaise; add other ingredients.

This can be used for sandwich spread or tomato stuffing.

Mrs. Edgar Witheow

# CHEESE SPREAD

3 packages cream cheese
2 small peppers
2 small onions
1 small bottle stuffed olives

Grind peppers, onions, and olives through meat chopper. Mix well with cheese. Mold on fancy plate and decorate with strips of peppers and thin olive slices. Chill and serve with crisp crackers.

Mrs. W. N. Palmer

# CLAM SPREAD

1 can minced clams
2 packages cream cheese

Drain clams (liquid can be used as cocktail). Chop clams finer if desired. Mix thoroughly with cheese and chill. Garnish with parsley or paprika.

Mrs. George D. Olds

# CRAB HORS D'OEUVRES

Arrange 1 teaspoon of crab meat on a cracker, top with 1 teaspoon homemade mayonnaise and heat in oven until it is slightly brown (15 minutes)

Mrs. William B. Shannahan

# MOCK PÂTÉ de FOIE GRAS

¼ pound liverwurst, unsliced
½ package cream cheese
¼ cup heavy cream
1 teaspoon Worcestershire
2 teaspoons prepared mustard
¼ teaspoon paprika, salt, pepper
⅛ cup sliced sautéed mushrooms

Skin liverwurst and mash with fork. Add the cream cheese, cream, and seasonings, and beat with silver fork until smooth and creamy. Add mushrooms. This serves 12 and is good spread on crisp crackers or canapé bases.

Mrs. William S. Pricher

## ASPARAGUS CANAPÉS

12 thin slices bread         mustard
6 thin slices boiled ham     mayonnaise
      12 asparagus tips

Trim crusts from bread; cut ham slices in half to fit bread. Spread with mustard. Dip asparagus in mayonnaise, place on ham with tip extending, roll slice of bread as for jelly roll and stick with toothpick at each end. Broil till toasted.

Mrs. Charles E. Wheeler

# BREADS
## and

# BISCUITS

# POTATO BREAD

2 cups diced potatoes, boiled
1½ cups potato water
1 tablespoon salt
2 tablespoons sugar
⅔ cup Crisco
1 cake yeast softened in
2 tablespoons lukewarm water

Press hot boiled potatoes through sieve and mix in all ingredients except yeast while hot. When lukewarm, stir in yeast and 2 cups sifted flour, beating well. Cover the sponge and place in warm place until double in bulk.

Mix in 5 or 6 cups sifted flour and work on board until it does not stick. Place in covered bowl and grease well.

When double in bulk, work down and form into loaves. Grease well, let rise until double in bulk again. Bake 1 hour in 350° oven.

I use small loaf pans to make a heavy crust. Some dough can be made into cloverleaf rolls, or put in icebox to be used later. Keep well greased.

Mrs. Wm T. Hammond

# CHEESE BREAD

1 3/4 cups milk - scalded

3 cups shredded sharp cheese

4 tablespoons sugar          1 package granular yeast

2 teaspoons salt          1/4 cup warm water

2 tablespoons butter          5 1/2 cups sifted flour

melted butter

Combine milk, 2 cups cheese, sugar, salt and butter. Stir until cheese melts. Cool. Sprinkle yeast over warm water, stir to blend. Add to milk mixture. Let stand 3 minutes. Add 5 cups of flour and 1 cup of cheese, mix well.

Turn out onto board which has been sprinkled with remaining flour. Knead until dough is smooth and satiny. Place in large bowl, brush with melted butter, cover and let rise until double in bulk, about 1 1/2 hours. Punch down and divide into thirds. Let rise 10 minutes covered with a towel. Shape into 3 loaves. Place in greased loaf pans. Cover and let rise until double in bulk. Bake 45 minutes in 375° oven.

Mrs. William B. Davis

# Extra Special Rolls

1 yeast cake dissolved with
1 tablespoon sugar
1 cup warm milk
1 cup butter, melted
1/2 cup sugar
3 eggs well beaten
1 Teaspoon salt
4 cups flour

Put warm milk, sugar and butter in bowl. Let cool. Beat eggs and add to above mixture, beaten eggs, yeast and flour. Let rise 4 hours, cut half and knead.

Roll thin, cover with melted butter, cut into 16 wedge shaped pieces. Roll into horns. Proceed the same for second half of dough. Let stand to rise 4 hours. Bake 10 minutes in 350° oven, decrease to 300°, bake 10 minutes more.

Mrs. L. Stuart Lankton

# GRANDMA SCOTT'S YEAST BREAD MIX

1 package granular yeast
1 cup milk
¼ cup sugar
1 teaspoon salt
¼ cup margarine
3½ cups flour
½ cup lukewarm water

Dissolve yeast in ½ cup lukewarm water for 10 minutes.

Scald the milk, and pour into a big mixing bowl. Add sugar, salt and margarine. Set aside to let sugar, etc., melt. Cool.

Add yeast. Beat in an egg. Add flour, stirring well. Cover the bowl with wax paper and a towel. Allow the dough to rise to double its bulk.

Form into desired shapes - parkerhouse, clover, etc., and let rise again until light.

Mrs. William Scott

# Jack Horner Rolls

2 cups flour, sifted
4 teaspoons baking powder
1 teaspoon salt
⅓ cup shortening
¾ cup milk
12-15 cooked prunes
brown sugar

Sift together flour, baking powder and salt. Cut in shortening. Add milk and stir until blended. Knead lightly on floured board. Roll about ¼ inch thick and cut into 2½ inch squares. Pit prunes. On each square place a pitted prune and 1 teaspoon brown sugar. Bring corners together over prunes, pinching edges to seal. Place in greased baking sheet and bake in oven (425°) about 25 minutes. Makes 12-15 rolls. Very nice for Tea and children love them.

Mrs. William I. Norris, Jr.

# STICKY BUNS

Roll dough (either made with the recipe
for white bread, or from the
prepared ready-mixed package,
and allow to rise once.)

1 cup brown sugar
1/4 pound butter or margarine
2 tablespoons corn syrup, light or dark
1/3 cup water
Cinnamon to taste
nut meats, pecan or walnuts

While dough is rising, boil the syrup
ingredients until slightly thick, and set
aside to cool.

Grease muffin tins, place several pieces
of nut meat in each tin and add about
1 teaspoon of the syrup.

When dough is ready to be shaped, roll
into oblong about 1/4 inch thick. Spread
with syrup and sprinkle with cinnamon.
Roll up and cut into slices across the
roll. Place cut side down in the muffin
tins, butter the tops slightly, and let rise
again until about double their size. (They
may be put in the refrigerator and allowed
to rise later in the day.)

## STICKY BUNS (continued)

Bake in a 375°-400° oven until tops are slightly brown. Remove and press the edges of the buns from the muffin tins. Turn tins upside down and the muffins will fall out as they cool.

This recipe gives enough syrup for 16 to 20 buns, or 1 package of roll mix.

Mrs. T. C. Kirby, jr.

# SHREDDED WHEAT BREAD

2 shredded whole-wheat biscuits
1 cup hot water
2 cups hot milk
3 Tablespoons lard (level)
3 tablespoons salt (level)
2 yeast cakes dissolved in ½ cup warm water
⅓ cup molasses
9 cups bread flour, sifted

Break shredded-wheat biscuits into combined hot water and milk. Mix well - then stir in lard, salt and molasses. Blend and when luke warm, crumble yeast cakes into lukewarm water and stir into the shredded-wheat mixture. Gradually beat in 4 cups of the flour and when thoroughly blended, stir in remaining flour. The amount of flour necessary will vary. Add more if needed to make a kneadable dough. Turn out on floured board. Dough will be sticky. Knead in only sufficient flour to work dough. Mixture should be smooth and elastic. Place dough in large greased mixing bowl, brush with melted lard and let rise in warm place until double in bulk. Punch it down, then let rise again. Form into 2 loaves and place in greased bread pans. Let rise until almost double in bulk. Bake at 375° for fifty to sixty minutes.

Lea Hazen

# Sally Lunn

1 cup milk
1 heaping tbsp. shortening
1 tbsp butter
3/4 cup warm water
1/2 yeast cake

1 egg, unbeaten
4 cups sifted flour

1 tsp. salt

Scald milk, add shortening and butter and let cool. Place warm water in a bowl and add sugar and yeast cake. Add milk mixture to bowl, add unbeaten egg, flour and salt. Beat 2 or 3 minutes and set aside to rise.

When light with bubbles on top, pour into well greased stem pan and let rise for 1 hour.

Preheat oven 350° and bake 30 minutes or until bread leaves side of pan, like cake.

When baked cut through the middle and fill with butter.

Sarah Adkins

# CRACKLING BREAD

2 cups water-ground cornmeal
1 teaspoon salt
3 teaspoons baking powder
½ cup skimmed milk
½ cup water
1 egg
½ or more cup cracklings

Mix and sift dry ingredients. Stir in milk and water and beat until smooth. Drop in egg and beat again. Stir in cracklings and bake in a lightly greased iron skillet about 30 minutes in a hot oven about 400 degrees.

Cracklings may be crushed with a rolling pin or broken into small pieces.

Mrs. George D. Olds

# SCOTCH SCONES

2 cups flour                          1 teaspoon salt
3 tablespoons baking powder    ⅓ cup milk
3 tablespoons shortening          2 eggs
2 tablespoons sugar                 raisins

Sift flour, baking powder, salt and sugar.
Add raisins. Add shortening and mix in lightly.
Beat eggs until light, add milk to eggs and
add slowly to mixture. Roll ½ inch thick on
floured board. Cut in 2 inch squares and
fold over, making them three cornered. Brush
with milk, dust with sugar. Bake in greased
pan 25 minutes in moderate oven.

Barbara Bromfield

# BRAN BREAD

2 cups wheat flour             3 teaspoons baking powder
2 cups bran                       ½ teaspoon salt
½ cup sugar                      1 egg
1 cup milk                         ¾ cup raisins
¾ cup chopped walnuts      1 tablespoon shortening

Mix and let rise 25 minutes. Bake 1 hour
in slow oven. Use loaf pan.

Mrs. Frank R. Clarke

# OATMEAL BREAD

2 cups boiling water
1 cup uncooked rolled oats
1 yeast cake
¼ cup lukewarm water
½ cup molasses
½ teaspoon salt
2 tablespoons melted shortening
5 cups sifted flour

Add boiling water to oats and let stand 1 hour. Dissolve yeast in the lukewarm water. Add molasses, salt, melted butter and yeast to oatmeal. Mix well and add flour a cup at a time, mixing after each addition. Add flour until dough does not stick to bowl. Put mixture in greased bowl and cover; let rise until double. Stir down and pour into greased pans; cover and let rise double. Bake in a hot oven - 425°- for 15 minutes, then at 375° for 30-35 minutes, until bread is brown and shrinks from pan.

Mrs. Harry Offutt

# MARYLAND BISCUITS

| (large quantity) | (small quantity) |
|---|---|
| 3 pounds flour | 3 cups flour |
| 6 ounces lard | 1/3 cup lard |
| 1 heaping tablespoon salt | 1/2 teaspoon salt |
| 1/2 teaspoon baking powder | 1/2 cup water or |
| 1 pint water | milk |

Blend flour and lard. Add salt and baking powder. Mix in the liquid.

Beat the dough with a hammer for 30 minutes. Form into small biscuits, prick top with fork and bake in a hot oven (500°).

Miss Addie Jefferson

There are various ways of beating these biscuits. One man recalls the sound of the cook beating biscuits with the nose of a hammer, out on a tree stump behind the kitchen. The flat of an axe, the heel of a sadiron, the heel of your hand, all these are mentioned in old recipes.

You must beat them until the dough blisters and is smooth-looking. You must beat them at least 30 minutes, and 45 minutes for company.

# QUEEN OF MUFFINS

⅓ cup butter
½ cup sugar or corn syrup
1 egg - well beaten
2 cups flour
4 teaspoons baking powder
3/4 cup milk

Cream the butter, add sugar gradually. Sift the flour and baking powder together. Add flour and milk alternately to butter - sugar mixture, stirring after each addition.

Bake in hot greased muffin tins for 25 minutes in 400° oven.

— Nita Henry Nevius

# CORN CAKES

3 cups of cornmeal
1 heaping tablespoon brown sugar or
2 tablespoons molasses
2 eggs
1 teaspoon salt
¼ cup melted butter
3 cups milk

Mix the above ingredients and add the milk gradually until you have a batter as thick as rich cream. Pour by tablespoonsful onto a hot griddle.

Mrs. R. S. Jones

---

# SPOON BREAD

Scald 2 cups corn meal, 1 teaspoon salt, enough boiling water to make a soft dough, about 2 cups. Add 1 tablespoon butter. Let cool. Add 3 eggs well beaten, mix well and add 1 pint milk, last of all 1 teaspoon baking powder. Cook in baking dish about 1 hour. 350° oven.

Mrs. J. F. Clark

# HUSH PUPPIES

2 cups corn meal
1 tablespoon flour
1 teaspoon soda
1 teaspoon baking powder
1 tablespoon salt
1 whole egg
6 tablespoons chopped onion
2 cups buttermilk

Mix all dry ingredients, add chopped onion, then milk and egg. Drop by spoonfulls into deep hot fat where fish are cooking. When done, they will float. Place on brown paper to drain.

This name originated around the campfire where they were toss-ed to the hounds to keep them quiet.

Mrs. Charles E. Wheeler

# BREAD CAKES

4-6 slices stale bread
1 egg
2 tablespoons milk
1 tablespoon melted shortening.
2 tablespoons sugar
½ teaspoon salt
2½ teaspoons baking powder.

Break bread in small pieces, place in strainer and sprinkle with hot water until soft. Place in pan; stir in ingredients and beat until light. Cook as you would hot cakes.

Josephine F. Miller

## FRESH OR CANNED CORN MUFFINS

1 cup corn          ⅔ cupful milk        3 eggs, beaten
½ teaspoon sugar    1 tablespoon baking powder

Add milk, sugar and eggs to corn. Mix and sift salt, flour and baking powder. Combine mixtures, drop by spoonsful into hot buttered muffin rings set in buttered baking pan. Bake in moderate oven until firm.

Mrs. W. Mitchell Price

# STEAMED PONE

4 cups milk
3 cups corn meal
2 cups flour
⅓ cup molasses
1 teaspoon soda
1 teaspoon salt

Mix well, pour in pudding mould and boil 3 hours. After removing from mould, place in warm oven to dry off.

Delia M. Mowbray

# Small Pancakes

1¼ cups flour
1 Teaspoon salt
3 eggs beaten
1 cup milk, very rich
2½ tablespoons melted butter
butter for frying

Sift flour with salt. To eggs
add a little milk and the melted
butter. Carefully beat in the flour
and the remaining milk. Allow
batter to stand for 1 hour or more.
Stir well before baking in pancake
pan. Do not bake pancakes too
brown.

Mrs. William L. Lane

# Old Fashioned Buckwheat Cakes

3 to 4 cups of buckwheat flour
¾ cup corn meal
½ cup white flour
1 teaspoon salt
¾ yeast cake dissolved in ½ cup warm
     water
1 quart warm water

Mix all the above ingredients and let stand in a warm place over night.

In the morning add 2 tablespoons black molasses and ½ teaspoon of baking soda dissolved in a spoonful of warm water.

Cook on a hot griddle. If the batter seems too thick, thin with warm water.

Mrs. John Schuyler

# CINNAMON TOAST

1 loaf sliced white bread
3 cups white sugar
1 pound butter
3 tablespoons cinnamon

Remove crusts from bread and cut each slice in thin strips, about 3 to a slice. Melt butter gently, and mix cinnamon and sugar together. Dip strips of bread in melted butter and then in sugar mixture, coating both sides completely.

Place on cookie sheet in 450° oven until they bubble and brown slightly. Remove and serve hot. Toast will be soft when first removed from oven, but will become crisp in a moment.

Will serve 20 at tea.

Louise Nash

# MRS. A.A. MILLER'S CRULLERS

3 eggs
1 cup milk
1 cup water
⅛ pound butter
¼ teaspoon salt
1½ cups sugar
1 teaspoon nutmeg
7-9 cups flour (approx.)
2 teaspoons baking powder for each
      cup of flour

Blend sugar and butter, add the slightly beaten eggs, milk and water. Mix in the flour and baking powder sifted together.

Roll to about ½ inch thick, cut, and fry in deep fat. Drain, and when a little cool shake crullers in a bag of sugar and cinnamon.

Mrs. Nita Henry Nevius

# Our Blueberry Waffles

| | |
|---|---|
| 1 cup sifted flour | 1 tablespoon sugar |
| 1 cup yellow cornmeal | 3 eggs, separated |
| 3 teaspoons baking powder | 1¼ cups milk |
| 1 teaspoon salt | 3 tablespoons melted |
| 1 cup blueberries | shortening |

Mix and sift flour, cornmeal, baking powder, salt and sugar. Add blueberries to dry mixture. Combine well-beaten egg yolks and milk; add to flour mixture and beat gently. Add shortening. Fold in stiffly beaten egg whites. Bake in hot waffle iron. Approximate yield: 7 waffles.

Mrs. John J. Shannahan, Jr.

=========================================

# Blueberry Muffins

| | |
|---|---|
| 1 cup flour | 1 egg, beaten |
| 2 teaspoons baking powder | 2 tablespoons melted shortening |
| ¼ teaspoon salt | 1 tablespoon cream (optional) |
| 1-2 tablespoons sugar | ½ cup blueberries |

Sift dry ingredients, add milk gradually, then beaten egg, shortening and berries. Bake in half-filled muffin pans at 375° until brown for 20 to 25 minutes.

Mrs. Elijah Nostrand

# Sweet Potato Biscuit

1 cup flour
3 tablespoons Crisco or other fat
½ teaspoon salt
1 cup sweet potatoes, boiled and
    put through sieve
½ cup milk
4 teaspoons level, baking powder

Sift dry ingredients. Beat melted shortening into sieved potatoes. Add milk. Add dry ingredients to potato mixture and work dough until smooth. Bat out to half an inch thick on floured board. Cut with biscuit cutter and bake in a hot oven 15 minutes.

Mrs. Douglas Hanks

"If your baking fails, burn a loaf".

# Date and Nut Muffins

3 eggs
1 cup sugar
1 cup pecan meats
1 package dates
3 tablespoons flour
1½ teaspoons baking powder
1 teaspoon vanilla

Cream sugar and egg yolks. Add flour and baking powder to dates and nuts (chopped). Beat egg whites stiff, add vanilla and fold into first mixture. Bake in 450° oven 15-20 minutes.

Makes 12 muffins. Serve with whipped cream.

Emily Ewing

# SWEET POTATO WAFFLES

4 tablespoons fat
1 tablespoon sugar
3/4 cup floor
1 egg
1 cup milk
1 cup mashed sweet potato
2 teaspoons baking powder
1 teaspoon salt
1/8 teaspoon cinnamon

Cream the fat and sugar. Add the well-beaten egg yolk, potato, milk and seasonings. Blend well. Fold in stiffly beaten egg white. Bake in a heated waffle iron until golden brown. Sprinkle with sugar and cinnamon.

Mrs. R. S. Jones

48

# BANANA BREAD

3 ripe bananas
½ cup sugar
2 eggs
2 cups flour
1 teaspoon salt
1 teaspoon soda
½ cup broken nut meats
2 tablespoons cold water

Crush bananas with a silver fork.
Add beaten eggs. Sift flour, salt and
soda together. Add sugar, then other
ingredients. Turn into greased loaf pan
and bake 1 hour in a slow oven 325°.

Mrs. Fred S. Munsell

# SOUTHERN RICE BREAD

Beat 1 egg until light. Add 1 cup milk,
½ teaspoon salt, 1 cup corn meal, 1 cup
cold boiled rice. Beat thoroughly, add
½ cup flour sifted with 3 teaspoons baking powder. Beat, stir in 4 tablespoons
milk. Pour into 3 greased cake pans,
bake in 350° oven 30 minutes. Spread
1st layer with butter, top with 2nd, more
butter, top 3rd layer with powdered
sugar.

Mrs. Mitchell Price

# Orange Biscuit

2 cups flour
4 Teaspoons baking powder
½ teaspoon salt
⅔ cup milk
4 tablespoons shortening
½ teaspoon grated orange rind
Juice of 1 orange

Mix and sift flour, baking powder and salt. Cut in shortening. Add orange rind and enough milk (about ⅔ cup) to make soft dough. Roll out on slightly floured surface to ½ inch thickness. Cut with biscuit cutter, dip half-size pieces of lump sugar in orange juice and place on biscuits. Bake in hot oven (425°) 15 minutes.

Mrs. E. P. Highley

# CRANBERRY AND ORANGE BREAD

2 cups flour
½ teaspoon salt
1½ teaspoons baking powder
⅛ teaspoon soda
1 cup sugar
Juice and rind of 1 orange
2 Tablespoons shortening
1 egg beaten
⅓ cup boiling water (about)
1 cup raw cranberries (chopped)
1 cup nutmeats (optional)
green cherries chopped (optional
    for Christmas coloring)

Sift together the dry ingredients.
To the juice of the orange and the
rind, add the shortening and enough
boiling water to make ¾ cup in all.
Add the beaten egg and then the
juice mixture to the dry ingredients.
Mix thoroughly. Add the cranberries,
nuts and chopped green cherries,
and bake in loaf pans in a hot
oven for about 1 hour. Store for
24 hours.

Mrs. John L. Downie

## ORANGE TEA BISCUITS

Sift 2 cups flour, 4 teaspoons baking powder and ½ teaspoon salt. Add the grated rind of 1 orange and ¼ cup shortening. When the shortening is cut in, add sufficient liquid to make a soft dough (about ⅔ cup diluted evaporated milk). Roll or pat out on a floured board and cut with small biscuit cutter. Place a piece of loaf sugar which has been dipped in orange juice in the center of each biscuit. Bake in a hot oven (450°) 15-17 minutes.

═══○══○══○══○═══

## SOUTHERN SOUR MILK BISCUITS

Sift 2 cups flour, ½ teaspoon soda, 1 teaspoon baking powder and 1 teaspoon salt. Cut in 4 tablespoons shortening and add 1 cup sour milk. Place dough on a floured board, roll or pat out ½ inch thick. Cut, and bake in a hot oven (450°) for 15-17 minutes.

Anne B. Perry

# NUT BREAD

2 cups white flour
2 cups graham flour
4 teaspoons baking powder
1 Cup sugar
1 egg
2 cups milk
1 cup nut meats

Sift flour once before measuring. Mix
and sift the dry ingredients. Add milk
and well beaten egg, mix thoroughly.
Add chopped nuts which have been
dredged in flour.

Pour into well greased pans. Let stand
20 minutes.

Bake in moderate oven 320° for 1 hour.

Yields 2 small loaves.

Mrs. John A. Schuyler

SOUPS

# OYSTER SOUP

1 quart oysters
2 tablespoons chopped celery
1 teaspoon chopped onion
1 sprig thyme
salt and pepper

Strain juice from oysters, saving liquor in saucepan. Add celery, onion, pepper and thyme to liquor and boil until vegetables are tender. Add oysters and cook until gills curl.

Thicken 1 pint milk with 1 tablespoon butter creamed with 1 tablespoon floor. When it is as thick as heavy cream, add oysters. Bring to a boil, take from stove, and add a slightly beaten yolk of egg.

Mrs. Robert G. Henry

# OYSTER BISQUE

1 pint oysters
1 slice onion
2 stalks celery
sprig parsley
bay leaf
1 quart milk
⅓ cup butter
⅓ cup flour
2 teaspoons salt
¼ teaspoon pepper

Drain oysters and chop. Add liquor and heat slowly to boiling. Scald milk with onion, parsley, celery, and bay leaf. Strain. Melt butter, blend in flour, add to milk and cook until thick stirring constantly. Add oysters. Serve immediately. Serves 6.

Mrs. Robert Valliant

# CRAB SOUP

2 quarts crab meat
2 quarts warm water
small bunch parsley - chopped
1 teaspoon red pepper
1 teaspoon black pepper
1 rounded tablespoon salt
¼ pound butter

Heat all ingredients in a pot, thicken with crushed crackers. (At Otwell they used flour rubbed with butter for thickening.)

When ready to serve, stir in 1 pint of cream.

Yields 1 gallon of soup.

Miss Martha Goldsborough

# CLAM BISQUE

1 dozen chowder clams (large)
onion
1 quart rich milk
thyme
pepper
minced parsley

Chop the clams in the meat chopper using
the finest cutter. Cook in water and clam
juice with the onion very slowly for 2 hours.

Mash through a sieve and discard hard
parts.

Add a quart of milk slowly and heat.
Add seasonings. Thicken slightly with
blended flour and milk.

Mrs. William T. Hammond

## CRAB SOUP

Steam 1 can claw meat in
3 tablespoons water. Add 1 quart
milk and butter size of egg. Salt,
pepper and cayenne.

Lizzie Cooper.

\\·//·\\·//·\\·//·\\·//·\\·//·\\·//·\\·//·\\·//·\\·//

## Mock CRAB BISQUE

| | |
|---|---|
| 1 can Tomato soup | 1 cup cream |
| 1 can pea soup | Seasoning to taste |
| 1 can water | |

Heat in double boiler. Add ½ pound backfin
crab. Add sherry and serve. Crab may
be replaced by lobster if desired.

Mrs. Norman Oyster

## CREOLE CRAB SOUP

    3 cans gumbo creole soup
    1 pound crab meat
    2 cans water
Mix, heat and serve.

Mrs. William Norris

# CLAM CHOWDER

50 chowder clams (makes about 1½ quarts chopped)

2 quarts water
1 quart diced potatoes
1 cup diced onions
3 tablespoons butter blended with
2 tablespoons flour
½ teaspoon black pepper
½ teaspoon thyme

Prepare clams by scrubbing well and steaming in a tightly covered cooker with 1 quart of water. Steam until the shells open wide.

Put the clams through a chopper, and add to the strained juice in which they were steamed.

Add the other ingredients and simmer 4 to 5 hours.

Mrs. William T. Hammond

This with a large green salad with carrot, celery, and radishes, etc. and melba toast makes a feast for clam lovers.

# MANINOSE CHOWDER

To prepare the maninose : scrub thoroughly to remove all mud and sand. Wash under running water. Let stand in cold water overnight to expell any sand.

2 dozen maninose, steamed, and juice
2 cups diced potatoes
1 large onion, diced
salt pork
3 cups cooked tomatoes
½ teaspoon salt
pepper and paprika
½ teaspoon thyme - or more

Saute the onion in the salt pork, add the diced potatoes and water the clams steamed in. Cook until the potatoes are almost done, add tomatoes and seasonings and cook again. Chop the maninose and add to the chowder, cook for a few minutes longer.

Mrs. William Myers, Jr.

# TURTLE SOUP

Choose a 5-6 pound turtle. Kill and wash well with stiff brush. Place in kettle of hot water, and let boil until the skin will come off easily — this means top of shell too. Place in kettle, cover with fresh water and let boil until top and lower shells come off easily. Save this water for soup. Be sure turtle is well cooked, as this is the only cooking it needs.

Now pick the turtle apart, being careful not to break the gall that is hidden inside liver. Cut the meat up with scissors and put it in the water. Hard boil 2 eggs, and cut up with meat. Season to taste with salt and prepared mustard.

Do not cook further until ready to serve, then heat, add 1/4 pound butter, and thicken slightly.

Mrs. E. T. Parsons

"Fatten the snapper in the hog's slop barrel."

# EAST INDIAN BISQUE

1 cup finely chopped onion
1 large apple
1½ cups cold water
1 cup chicken consomme
½ cup heavy cream
⅛ Teaspoon curry powder
¼ Teaspoon salt

Combine onion and apple in water, cook until Tender. Add consomme and bring to a boil, cook Ten minutes. Add hot mixture slowly to the cream. Season with curry and salt, return to heat and cook one minute longer. Serve immediately.

Mrs. Zebulon Stafford


"After breakfast, work awhile;
After dinner; sit awhile;
After supper; walk a mile."

# CREAM OF TOMATO SOUP

1½ cups of water
2 tablespoonsful minced onion
1 tablespoonful minced parsley
½ bay leaf
2 whole cloves
1 teaspoonful celery salt
2 cups ripe tomatoes, sliced
2 cups thin cream
4 tablespoonsful whipped cream

Place all ingredients except cream in sauce pan and simmer for twenty minutes. Heat to boiling point. Heat cream separately, to boiling point. When ready to serve, beat hot cream slightly and stir in slowly. Garnish each serving with one tablespoonful of whipped cream, dusted lightly with paprika.

Mrs. R. Hammond Gibson

## Old.fashioned Italian Minestrone

Finely chop about 1/4 pound salt pork,
1/4 pound cured ham and a sprig
of parsley. Add to about 2 quarts
of cold water, and bring to the
boiling point.

Add:  1 cup well washed rice
      2 stalks minced celery
      1 onion
      1 diced carrot
      1 peeled tomato
      1/4 head sliced hard cabbage
      1/2 pound shredded string beans

Simmer for about an hour.

Add:  1/2 pound tender green peas
      1 diced potato
      1 diced tender squash

Continue cooking for another hour.
Season to taste with salt and pepper.

Add:  3 tablespoons Parmesan
      cheese just before remou-
      ing from the stove.

Mrs. Frank Gregson

# BUTTER BEAN SOUP AND SLIPPERY DUMPLINGS

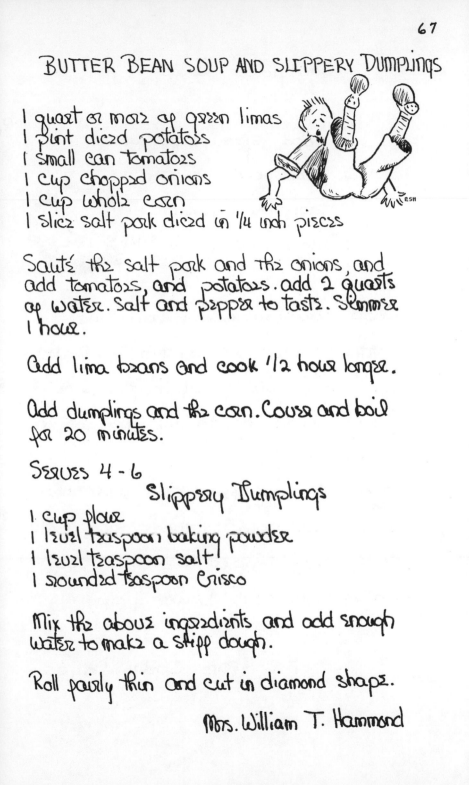

1 quart or more of green limas
1 pint diced potatoes
1 small can tomatoes
1 cup chopped onions
1 cup whole corn
1 slice salt pork diced in 1/4 inch pieces

Sauté the salt pork and the onions, and add tomatoes, and potatoes. add 2 quarts of water. Salt and pepper to taste. Simmer 1 hour.

Add lima beans and cook 1/2 hour longer.

Add dumplings and the corn. Cover and boil for 20 minutes.

SERVES 4 - 6

## Slippery Dumplings

1 cup flour
1 level teaspoon baking powder
1 level teaspoon salt
1 rounded teaspoon Crisco

Mix the above ingredients and add enough water to make a stiff dough.

Roll fairly thin and cut in diamond shape.

Mrs. William T. Hammond

# Cauliflower Soup

1 good sized cauliflower
2 tablespoons butter
1 tablespoon flour
2 egg yolks

Cook cauliflower and save the water it has been boiled in. Make a cream sauce of butter and flour, using the cauliflower water. Cook thoroughly.
Beat 2 egg yolks and add the soup gradually to them, but don't cook any longer. Serve in soup plates with cauliflower flowerets.

Mrs. Ogden Driggs —

# VEGETABLE SOUP

1 pound shin beef with bone
3½ quarts cold water
2½ tablespoons salt
1 clove minced onion
4 Tablespoons minced parsley
⅛ Teaspoon pepper
1 cup cut-up stringbeans
¾ cup diced celery
⅔ cup shredded cabbage
⅔ cup shelled peas
1 cup diced carrots
1 #2 can tomatoes (2½ cups)

Combine beef, water and two tablespoons salt. Cover, bring to a boil, skim, recover and simmer four hours. Remove bone and meat. Add remaining ingredients except two tablespoons parsley. Cover and simmer 30 minutes, sprinkle with remaining parsley, add meat and serve.

Mrs. Robert G. Henry, Jr.

## Tomato Bouillon

1 quart can tomatoes
2 cans bouillon
1 can consomms
1 dozen whole cloves
1 tsp. celery seed
2 onions, chopped fine
juice of 1/2 lemon
2 bay leaves
little Tabasco sauce

Boil tomatoes, onion, cloves, celery seed
and bay leaves for 30 minutes. Strain
through a jelly bag, add bouillon, consomms
lemon juice and tabasco sauce.
Serve hot with a thin slice of lemon.
To serve jellied, add one envelope of
unflavored gelatine soaked in 1/2 cup cold
water.

Mrs. John K. Todd

# SEA FOOD

72

# MARYLAND OYSTER ROAST

The best oysters for roasting are of medium size. Allow a dozen oysters per person, although experience may prove your calculations low.

Preparation: Hose off or scrub off all the mud and clay from the oyster shells. Have a piece of wire netting stretched across the open fire. One inch or inch and a half wire mesh will do. Be sure it is firmly anchored at the sides. Lay the oysters on the netting — don't pile them up. Turn occasionally by shaking the wire.

When the oyster shells open — they are done. Equip each guest with a pot holder and oyster fork. Serve with drawn butter or barbeque sauce, if desired.

# Rough and Ready Oysters

1 qt. select oysters

### Sauce:

½ lb. butter           ⅛ tsp. paprika

1 tsp. English mustard 2 tsp. celery salt

1 tbl. Worchestershire Sauce

4 tbs. Catsup

Heat drained oysters in top of double boiler until their edges curl.

Melt butter, mix in the other ingredients and heat until piping hot. Pour over oysters.

Serves 6.

Mrs. P. Kenard Wright

# OYSTERS CASINO

1 pint oysters
3 slices bacon, chopped
4 tablespoons onion, chopped
2 tablespoons green pepper, chopped
1 teaspoon lemon juice
½ teaspoon salt
½ teaspoon pepper
½ teaspoon Worcestershire
2 dashes Tobasco

Fry bacon, add onion, green pepper, celery, and cook until tender. Add seasonings and mix well. Arrange drained oysters on buttered baking dish. Spread bacon mixture over oysters. Bake in 350° oven about 10 minutes

Mrs. R. S. Jones

# CHESAPEAKE OYSTER LOAF

1 loaf French bread
2 dozen oysters
½ cup cream
1 tablespoon chopped celery
2 dashes Tabasco
salt and pepper

Cut off top crust of a loaf of French bread and scoop out inside. Butter ⅓ of the scooped-out portion and toast in oven.

Fry 2 dozen oysters in butter, add ½ cup cream, celery, salt and pepper and Tabasco, and the toasted bread.

Fill hollowed loaf with this mixture. Cover with top crust and bake 20 minutes, basting frequently with liquor from oysters. Slice and serve hot.

The oysters may be served in individual hard crusted rolls if desired.

Mrs. Robert C. Morris

# FRIED OYSTERS

1 quart oysters
2 eggs
2 tablespoons milk
1 teaspoon salt
⅛ teaspoon pepper
1 cup bread or cracker crumbs

Drain oysters. Beat eggs, milk and seasonings. Dip oysters in crumbs, then in eggs, then in crumbs again. If oysters are small press several together in palm of hand after crumbing.

Fry in hot fat.

Mrs. Robert Valliant

# GLORIFIED OYSTERS

1 pint oysters, drained
1 teaspoon Worcestershire sauce
¼ pound crackers, rolled fine
salt, pepper
1 can condensed mushroom soup
2 tablespoons butter
1 outside stalk celery

Place layer of oysters in bottom of buttered casserole. Season with salt and pepper and Worcestershire sauce. Cover with layer of cracker crumbs. Repeat until oysters are used. Pour on condensed mushroom soup and press down with spoon. Top with cracker crumbs and dot with butter. Lay celery stalk on top. Bake in moderate oven (350°) for twenty minutes. Remove celery. Place under broiler to brown. Serves four generously.

Katherine Harrison

"If you would catch oysters, sing
If fish ---- be still."

# Oyster Fritters Hawaiian

4 eggs, separated
1 tablespoon minced scallions
1/2 teaspoon salt
1/8 teaspoon pepper
6 tablespoons flour
1 cup chopped, drained oysters

Beat egg yolks until thick and lemon-colored. Add scallions, salt and pepper. Fold in flour, a little at a time. Fold in oysters and stiffly beaten egg whites. Fry by spoonfuls in a little hot fat. Approximate yield: 4-6 portions.

Mrs. H. V. L. Bloomfield

---

# Oyster Pie

1 quart of oysters, drained
pepper, salt and butter to taste

Place between 2 short crusts with lumps of butter on top one. Bake in moderately hot oven.

Mrs. Alonzo Elliott

# BARBECUED OYSTERS

Open large fat oysters in deep shell, allowing 6 for each person. Place opened oysters on baking sheet, sprinkle each lightly with cracker crumbs, and add 1 teaspoon sauce for each oyster.

Sauce for 24 oysters:

½ cup melted butter
½ teaspoon paprika
juice of ½ lemon
salt if needed

Bake in 450° oven until crumbs brown and oyster edges curl but not until dry. Serve HOT.

Mrs. William T. Hammond

# CHRISTMAS DAY OYSTER STEW

1 quart oysters and liquid with them
1 cup water
2 stalks celery
1 cup undiluted evaporated milk
2 cups whole milk
lump of butter
1/8 teaspoon nutmeg
1/8 teaspoon ground cloves
1/8 teaspoon pepper
1 1/2 teaspoons salt

Cut up celery fine and boil it several minutes in water. Add 1 quart oysters and the liquid that is with them and boil until edges curl. Add the milk, butter and dry ingredients.

Edith Adkins

# PICKLED OYSTERS

Strain the oysters from the liquor and put the liquor on to boil with salt, whole grain of pepper, blades of mace, and a very little all spice.

Wash the oysters in cold water and when the spiced liquor is boiling, put in oysters and cook until the edges curl.

Strain the oysters from the liquor and put in a dish to cool. When both liquor and oysters are cold, add a cup of white wine and a cup of vinegar for every gallon of oysters. Add the oysters and they are ready to serve.

A very old recipe of Aunt Mary Goldsborough's of Otwell.

Miss Martha Goldsborough

# OYSTERS AND MACARONI, AU GRATIN

1 pint oysters
3 tablespoons butter
3 tablespoons flour
1½ cups milk
1 cup cooked macaroni
1 teaspoon salt
⅛ teaspoon pepper
1 cup grated cheese

Drain oysters. Melt butter in top of double boiler, blend in flour, add milk and cook until thick, stirring constantly.

Place layer of macaroni in a buttered casserole, cover with a layer of oysters. Sprinkle with salt, pepper, and grated cheese. Repeat layer. Pour sauce over contents of casserole, top with grated cheese.

Bake in moderate oven for 30 minutes, or until brown.

Mrs. Robert Valliant

# OYSTERS ROCKEFELLER

1½ pints oysters, or 36
2 cups cooked spinich
4 tablespoons onion
2 bay leaves
1 tablespoon parsley
½ teaspoon celery salt
½ teaspoon salt
6 drops Tobasco
6 tablespoons butter

Place shucked, drained oysters on deep half of shell. Put spinich, onion, bay leaves, parsley through food chopper. Add seasonings to spinich and cook in butter for 5 minutes. Add bread crumbs and mix. Spread mixture over oysters and bake in hot oven for 10 minutes. Garnish with lemon slices.

Oysters may be placed in a casserole instead of shells if desired.

Mrs. R. S. Jones

# SCALLOPED OYSTERS

Pick, wash and drain 1 solid quart oysters. Place in layers in baking dish, alternately with dry bread or cracker crumbs and seasonings.

When dish is filled add the strained oyster liquor and sufficient milk to moisten. Cover with crumbs, add 1 tablespoon butter in bits, and bake ½ hour in hot oven.

Mrs. Mary Carroll

# CLAM PIE

Rich pastry for top crust. No bottom
crust is used.

    1 dozen hard clams (minced) Save juice
    finely chopped parsley to taste
    1 green pepper (ground)
    ¼ pound finely diced bacon
    1 good sized white onion, sliced
    2 large white potatoes, sliced
    pepper and salt to taste

Cook potatoes and onions together
until tender, using as little water as
possible.

Grease eight inch shallow pie dish lightly
and fill with layers of first potato and
onion, then clam, pepper, seasonings, bacon
and parsley, repeating until dish is full.

Cover with crust and bake until crust is
golden brown. This pie is better the day
after it is made, reheated.

                    Mrs. Ralph Wiley

# DEVILED CLAMS #1

4 dozen clams, ground fine
1 tiny clove garlie
1 cup bread crumbs
1 small onion, chopped fine
Worcestershire
Parsley or chives
2 tablespoons flour
½ teaspoon dry mustard

Place clams and juice in pan, and let come to a boil. Cut up onion and garlie, place in pan, and cook in butter. Add flour, pour in clam juice gradually. Add bread crumbs, chives or parsley, and seasonings. Add clams. Fill the shells, coat with beaten egg and dip in bread crumbs. Place under broiler and broil slowly.

Mrs. Thomas M. Carpenter

# DEVILED CLAMS #1

6 onions
¼ pound of butter

Cook this while preparing
50 clams, chopped fine. Then
add to onions:

2 bunches parsley
5 eggs, beaten
1 pint of bread crumbs

Mix all. Wet with one egg and
cover with crumbs after placing
in individual shells. Bake one
hour in slow oven.

                    Willard G. Rouse

# MANINOSE FRITTERS

1 pint maninose, ground
1 tablespoon butter, melted
2 eggs, beaten
1/4 cup milk
1/4 teaspoon baking powder
flour, pepper, salt

Put whole maninoses through the meat grinder. Add eggs and milk. Dredge in enough flour to make batter of pancake consistency. Add seasoning to taste. Lastly sprinkle on and stir in the baking powder. Cook on a hot griddle.

Mrs. Bryan Smith

# CRAB À LA TALBOT

1 pound crabmeat
1 cup milk
1 egg yolk
2 tablespoons butter

2 cups corn
2 chopped green peppers
1 small onion chopped
salt and pepper (red)

Brown onion in butter, add milk, corn and peppers. When corn is cooked, add crabmeat, salt and red pepper. Heat and mix thoroughly, add beaten egg yolk and stir until thick. Serve on toast.

Patricia C. Wrightson

# STEAMED MANINOSE

Soak maninose in wash tub of water a day or two, changing water often. Thus they will rid themselves of sand.

Bring to a boil 1 cup water in a large pot, add 1 stalk of celery, bay leaf and small amount thyme. Dump in the clams, sprinkle with salt and pepper and clamp on the lid.

Let them steam until done - not very long. They make lots of juice, so serve in large soup plates; clams, juice, shells and all. Serve melted butter on the side to dunk the clams in.

Carroll M. Elder

# MARYLAND DEVILED CRABS

8 cleaned crab shells
1 pound crab meat
3 tablespoons butter
2 tablespoons flour
1 cup milk
1 cup bread crumbs
1 teaspoon salt
1 teaspoon dry mustard
⅛ teaspoon cayenne
⅛ teaspoon nutmeg
parsley

Mix bread crumbs with crabmeat. Make a sauce of butter, flour and milk Add seasonings. Mix the sauce with crabmeat and crumbs. Cool, then fill the shells with crab mixture. Sprinkle with bread crumbs and bake in 400° oven for 15 minutes.

Mrs. D. C. Kirby

# A MARYLAND CRAB FEAST

Use 2½ dozen large hard shell crabs for 6 people. Wash live crabs with a hose if necessary. A lard can with tight fitting lid is a good container for steaming – holding just 2½ dozen. Put grating in bottom of pan, add 3 cups vinegar, 4 tablespoons salt, 4 tablespoons dry mustard, 4 teaspoons black pepper, 1 teaspoon red pepper and 1 teaspoon Tobasco. When this is boiling rapidly, put in the crabs - kicking vigorously. When steam rises hard count time for 20 minutes. The crabs will turn bright red.

Spread a table with a thick layer of newspapers. Provide each guest with a paring knife, nut cracker or heavy handled knife to break claws. Paper towels and beer.

Every man for himself now. A tray of steamed crabs in the center of the table. Remove the top shell, feelers, apron and discard the gray-white spongy "dead men's fingers" and the intestines. Break the claw shell and split the body to get at the meat. Don't neglect the greenish crab fat — it is a delicacy.

# CRAB CAKES #1

1 cup rich milk
3 tablespoons butter
3 tablespoons flour
1 egg
½ teaspoon salt
dash Tabasco
¼ teaspoon dry mustard
1 tablespoon Worcestershire
1 tablespoon fresh chopped parsley
Generous grating nutmeg
1 pound crab meat

Make white sauce of butter, flour, milk, and salt. Just before removing from fire, stir in whole egg, cook 1 minute, then add seasonings. Allow to cool.

Pick over 1 pound crab meat to remove shell. Add crab to sauce, mix thoroughly but gently. When cold, form into large cakes, dip in bread crumbs and fry in butter.

These cakes are quite soft, and if preferred, the mixture can be baked in ramekins or a casserole.

Betty Jean Wheeler

# Crab Cakes #2

| | |
|---|---|
| 4 slices bread | 1 teaspoon Worcester- |
| ½ cup olive oil | shire sauce |
| ⅛ teaspoon dry mustard | 2 eggs |
| ½ teaspoon salt | 1 tablespoon chopped |
| 1 dash paprika | parsley |

1 pound crab flakes

1 pound claw meat

Trim crusts from bread, lay in flat tin or platter and pour olive oil over them. Let stand one hour. Pull apart lightly with two forks. To the small bits of bread add seasonings, yolks of eggs and crab meat. Mix lightly with a fork, fold in stiffly beaten egg whites and shape into about 18 cakes. Brown in a hot skillet just brushed with fat.

— Mrs. Howard Bloomfield

# CRAB CECEL

2 tablespoons butter
2 tablespoons flour

Warm and smooth to paste.

add

2 eggs beaten well with
2 cups milk.

Cook until slightly thick

add

1 teaspoon curry powder
2 tablespoons tomato catsup
2 ounces sherry
salt, pepper, paprika to taste.

add

1 pound white lump crab meat.

Heat thoroughly, serve very
hot. Can be served in casserole or individual bowls,
on toast, or hot swiebach.

Mrs. C. D. Cox.

# CRAB IMPERIAL

2 cups crab meat
2 tablespoons butter
2 tablespoons flour
1 cup milk
1 teaspoon dry mustard
1 teaspoon salt
⅛ teaspoon nutmeg (optional)
2 teaspoons minced parsley
2 teaspoons lemon juice
½ cup cracker crumbs

Make a sauce of flour, butter
and milk. Add all seasonings
and crab meat and mix well.
Fill six crab shells and top with
cracker crumbs. Bake in 350°
oven until brown and serve
hot garnished with lemon and
parsley. This can also be
baked in a casserole.

Mrs. Carroll C. Elliott

# CRAB EVERGREEN

1/4 pound butter or margarine
1 wedge pimento cheese
1 small can mushrooms
1 can evaporated milk
1 pound crabmeat
1 box elbow macaroni

Melt butter in double boiler. Cut cheese up into butter. Stir until melted. Add the can of mushrooms with the juice. Let all this simmer for 5 minutes. Add the evaporated milk and when all this is hot, add the crabmeat, which has been picked over.
Cook the macaroni.

Put the crabmeat and the macaroni in layers in a casserole dish and bake for 20 minutes in moderate oven.

Mrs. Adolp Koehn

# DEVILED SOFT SHELL CRABS

Quantity - 1 dozen.

2  heaping tablespoons parsley
2  tablespoons onion
2  teaspoons paprika
3  ounces lemon juice
3  ounces sherry wine

Clean crabs and blot dry with paper toweling. flour well just before putting in skillet. Use large skillet with tight lid. Have bottom covered with 1/4 inch fat- half butter is preferable. Place crabs in skillet, one layer deep, salt and pepper well. Sift dehydrated parsley and onion flakes over crabs and redden well with paprika. When very hot pour lemon juice over and cover tightly. See that crabs do not stick and replenish if necessary. When browned turn over and sprinkle again with parsley, onions, paprika, salt and pepper and cover. When browned on bottom pour sherry wine over them. Cover for three minutes and serve immediately.

Mrs. B. M. Bates

# SOFT SHELL CRABS

Clean, wash and dry well. Cover crabs with flour, salt and pepper and fry in small amount of fat over a very moderate flame for 15 or 20 minutes. Drain on absorbent paper.

(Some Eastern Shore cooks parboil crabs a few minutes before frying — this gives them a well cooked flavor and cuts down on frying time.)

Virginia . C. Cover.

# CORNED SHAD.

Split shad and remove backbone. Mix salt, pepper and 4 tablespoons brown sugar. Sprinkle on shad which is skin side down on a lightly greased broil and serve platter. Let stand several hours, then broil 8 to 10 minutes. Shad can also be fried or baked.

Edith Adkins

# CRAB NORFOLK

1 can crab meat       salt
¼ pound butter      red and ████ pepper
     1¼ tablespoons vinegar

Mix seasonings with crabmeat gently. Place in casserole, dot with butter, cover, and bake in oven 350° for 20 - 30 minutes.

Samuel S. Sands

# CRAB FOX HARBOR

3 pounds lump crab     1 teaspoon salt
1 teaspoon dry mustard    1 teaspoon pepper
1 tablespoon grated onion   ½ cup milk (rich)
     ½ cup mayonnaise

Mix all together lightly and put in casserole. Sprinkle with bread crumbs, dot with butter. Bake in 400° oven for 30 minutes. Serves 8
Delicious served with tomato aspic.

Mrs. John G. Shannahan, Jr.

# TOSSED CRAB

1 pound crabmeat
1/4 pound butter or margarine
1/2 teaspoon dry mustard
1/2 teaspoon lemon juice
paprika, salt, pepper to taste

Flake 1 pound crabmeat into serving bowl.
Melt butter or margarine. Add seasoning
and lemon juice. Pour over cold crab
and toss to distribute sauce over meat.

Mrs. Ralph Wiley

# CRAB MEAT AU GRATIN

Melt:
        1 tablespoon butter
        2 tablespoons flour, mix to-gether

Add:
        1-16 ounce can mushroom soup
            Stir until thick

Add:
        6 1/2 ounce crab meat
        1 1/2 cups soft bread crumbs
        1/4 teaspoon salt
        dash pepper
        1 cup grated cheese
Put in buttered dish and cook in oven
until hot and slightly browned.

Mrs. J. H. Ross

# CODFISH BALLS

1 cup raw salt codfish
1 pint raw potatoes cliced
1 egg well beaten
salt and pepper to taste

Put potatoes and fish in stew pan. Cover with boiling water, and cook until potatoes are tender.

Drain, mash, and add beaten egg.

Form into balls and fry in deep hot fat.

— Mr. Richard Goldsborough

# Crimped Cod or Halibut

1½ pounds halibut or cod cutlets
4 cups water
1½ teaspoons salt
1 teaspoon vinegar

Place fish cutlets in the 4 cups water
to which has been added the 1½ teaspoon
salt and the vinegar and let stand for
3 hours.

1 onion quartered
1 small bay leaf
2 black peppercorns
½ teaspoon salt
3 cups water

Combine and boil together the onion,
bay leaf, peppercorns, salt and water. Lace
fish in boiling water, lower flame and
simmer for about 10 minutes. Serve on
hot platter. Decorate with sprigs of
parsley and skins of lemon. On side
serve shrimp sauce. Serves 4.

Mrs. Francis G. Bartlett

To boiling fish add a tablespoon of
vinegar. It prevents crumbling, and
adds flavor.

# FISH À LA QUEEN ANNE

1 pound flaked cooked fish
4 chopped cooked mushrooms
1 tablespoon chopped parsley
1 cup milk or cream
1 egg yolk
1 tablespoon butter
1 tablespoon flour
salt, pepper, and sherry

Melt butter, stir in flour, add milk and bring to a boil; stir until smooth. Then add fish, mushrooms, salt and pepper. When thoroughly heated, add beaten egg yolk and parsley. Mix well and add 1 tablespoon or more sherry as you take it from fire. Serve in shells or ramekins.

Patricia C. Wrightson

## Scallops Newburg

1 pound (1 pint) scallops
2 tablespoons butter
¼ cup Sherry
2 tablespoons Brandy

3 egg yolks beaten slightly
½ cup thin cream
½ teaspoon salt

Cayenne

Rinse and drain scallops; cover with cold water. Heat slowly to boiling and drain.
Cook scallops in butter 3 minutes, breaking into small pieces as you stir.
Add Sherry and Brandy and cook 1 minute longer.
Mix egg yolks and cream. Add to scallops and cook just until mixture thickens, stirring constantly. (If over-cooked, sauce will curdle) Remove from heat immediately, season with salt and cayenne and serve on toast or crackers, or in patty shells. (Perfect for the chafing dish) Serves 3    — Margaret H. Gregson

# PICKLED HERRING

Clean carefully 12-14 herring and wipe very dry. Fit a layer of fish in bottom of stone baking crock and sprinkle with salt, red pepper and whole cloves. Add layer of fish and seasonings, and repeat until crock is well filled.

Pour the best cider vinegar over fish to cover. Place crock lid on, or tie greased paper on tightly.

Bake in slowest oven possible for 24 hours or more, or until vinegar is nearly absorbed and bone is dissolved. The crock can be taken in and out of oven if necessary.

Mrs. William T. Hammond

# KEDGEREE

fish, cooked and broken up
rice, boiled
yolks of hard-boiled eggs, chopped fine
melted butter
salt, pepper and curry is desired

Mix the fish, rice and egg yolks. Salt
and pepper to taste. Toss in melted
butter to which curry has been added.
Serve hot. This is a wonderful dish
if you have left-over fish and rice.

Mrs. R. Howe Lagarde

\\\ /// \\\/// \\\/// \\\/// \\\ /// \\\/// \\\ /// \\\/// \\\ /// \\\

# HOT LOBSTER SANDWICHES

1 can lobster                    mayonnaise
3 lettuce leaves (chopped)   finger rolls

To lobster and lettuce leaves add enough
mayonnaise to soften. Season to taste.
Mix well. Pile high on split and
buttered finger rolls and broil until
quite hot and toasty.

Mrs. Durrie B. Hardin

# SNAPPER STEW

To dress a snapper:

Cut off head and bleed well. Then scrub very well with stiff brush. Run a sharp knife around each shell and skin out the legs and cut off toes. Separate shells and take out all meat and bone this. Remove gall from liver carefully.

Put shell, skin, and bones in a pot with 2 stalks celery, 1 carrot, 1 large onion, 1 clove garlic, thyme, bay leaf, parsley, salt and pepper.

Simmer this in enough water to cover well for a couple of hours. Strain.

Meanwhile, cut up the meat into small pieces and brown well in butter in heavy pot. Sprinkle with flour and brown again. Pour over this the stock and let simmer until turtle meat is tender. Just before serving add 2 or 3 hard boiled eggs sliced. Pour a glass of Sherry or Madeira in your soup tureen and then add stew.

Carroll M. Elder

# TERRAPIN

Use from 5½ inches up — these are females and have eggs in varying amounts. Wash well in cold water, using a stiff brush. Plunge in boiling water and cook until toe nails pull out easily. Pry off both shells and put same back in the water (also bones during picking) and boil down to about a half.

Disseet, using all but head, nails and intestines. Cut meat across grain with scissors. Cut gall sac from the liver with great care — if it breaks, wash well immediately. Remove 1 layer of skin from legs and sac from eggs. The greater the care in picking, the more meat and the less bones you have.

Put meat, liver, heart and eggs in jar with enough liquor to seal. Save twice as much liquor.

To serve: heat thoroughly (never allow to boil) in flat pan, using cake turner or shaking pan. Do not stir. Add as much liquor as desired, salt, pepper, cayenne to taste, and ½ pound butter per quart of meat.

Serve Sherry or Madeira in a glass, not in terrapin.

Donald S. Ross

# TURTLE À LA KING

6 hard-cooked eggs
2 tablespoons butter
2 cups light cream
½ teaspoon salt
dash pepper
dash allspice
dash nutmeg
2 cups chopped cooked turtle meat

Force egg yolks through sieve, then cream yolks with butter. Scald cream over hot water, add seasonings and beat in egg yolk-butter mixture. Add turtle, cover and cook 10 minutes, or until heated. Serve hot, garnished with white of egg. Serves 6.

# BAKED ROCK FISH

Have 4-5 pound rock cleaned, and head and tail removed. Score each side in about 4 places, and season inside and out with salt and pepper.

Place fish on well greased baking pan and place a strip of cured ham or bacon in each gash. Surround fish with 3 medium sized potatoes, 2 large carrots, and 2 onions, pared and cut in wedges; and a few strips of green pepper. Add 1 cup of water and 1 teaspoon salt over vegetables, and place in 550° oven. Cook for 15 minutes, remove and baste with:

1/4 cup melted butter or oil
1 teaspoon creole powder
juice of 1/2 lemon

Baste all often and add enough water to have 1 cup of sauce when done. Cook for 1 hour 15 minutes. Serve thickened sauce in sauce boat. Serves 4-6.

Mrs. William T. Hammond

# BOILED ROCK FISH WITH SAUCE

2 or 3 pound Rockfish - cleaned

Sauce:
1½ - 2 cups white sauce
1 teaspoon lemon juice - or to taste
dash red pepper
¼ cup capers
½ teaspoon worcestershire sauce (optional)
¾ teaspoon salt and pepper
4 hard boiled eggs

Place cleaned rockfish in cheese cloth, tie closed and drop in boiling salted water to which has been added - a slice of onion, 2 whole cloves, carrot, bay leaf, 2 peppercorns. Boil 6 to 10 minutes per pound. Lift out of water carefully and place on large platter before removing cheesecloth. Make the sauce before starting to prepare the fish, and then pour sauce over fish and garnish the platter with slices of hard boiled eggs, lemon wedges and parsley.

Another garnish to use with rock is to render 6 or 8 slices of bacon which have been diced into small pieces and pour the hot bacon grease and rendered bacon over the boiled rockfish. This recipe serves 4.

Mrs. James Trippe Ferguson

# BAKED SHAD

Make a dressing of bread crumbs, butter, salt, pepper, and a little celery, onion and pimento. Stuff the body of the fish and sew it up. Score the upper part of the fish with a sharp knife and sprinkle the whole fish with salt, pepper, paprika and flour. Place on a greased broiler rack and bake in a 350° oven 15 minutes to the pound. Baste, if necessary with butter melted in hot water.

Virginia C. Cover

### Quick Curry

1 can mushroom soup (condensed)

1 can grated Tuna fish

1 Teaspoon curry powder
    (must be Wagner's)

2 cups cooked rice

Mix well. Bake 20 minutes

A package of frozen peas or canned peas may be added to this.

Mrs. Frank Gregson -

# PANNED SHAD ROE WITH BACON AND MUSHROOMS

Parboil 2 roes 5 minutes in acidulated water. Drain, plunge into cold water.

Fry 8 strips of bacon and put on a hot platter. Saute the roe in the bacon fat, until well browned on both sides. Transfer to the hot platter, keeping it hot.

Cook in the frying pan ½ pound mushrooms cut in halves, ¾ cup water, ½ teaspoon Worcestershire sauce, salt, paprika, ½ teaspoon of Kitchen bouquet, and blend in 1 tablespoon flour. Stir constantly until sauce is smooth, add a few drops of lemon juice. Pour the mushroom gravy over the shad roe and lay the bacon on top. Garnish with parsley or watercress.

Mrs. S. N. Hersloff

"Shad appear when the shadblow blooms"

# Shrimp Sea Island

Marinate in a highly seasoned French Dressing, any amount of cooked deveined shrimp in your hydrator for twenty-four hours. Do add plenty of sliced Bermuda onions - Bay leaves and capers are optional. Serve, as is, in the dressing with plenty of tooth-picks. Perfect with cocktails.

Mrs. Harry S. Rossiter, Jr.

∿∿∿∿∿∿∿∿∿∿∿∿∿∿∿∿∿∿∿

# Pickled Shrimp

| | |
|---|---|
| 2 pounds shrimp | 1 teaspoon dry mustard |
| 1¾ cups vinegar | 1 teaspoon celery seed |
| 1¼ cups water | 1 teaspoon black pepper |
| 1 tablespoon salt | Several dashes red pepper |
| 3 large onions, sliced | |

Combine all ingredients except shrimp. Bring brine to boil. Add shrimp 1 pound at a time so liquid doesn't cool too much. Boil each batch shrimp five to eight minutes. When two rounds of shrimp finished, pour brine over shrimp, store in refrigerator in glass, enamel or porcelain container. Serve as is after twelve hours.

Katharine Harrison

# SHRIMP LOUISIANE

1 pound shrimp
1 tablespoon butter
1 tablespoon flour
4 tomatoes (or 1 small can)
1 cup water
1 onion, green pepper, parsley, shallot tops
pepper, salt, cayenne
½ tablespoon of Worcestershire

Chop the onion fine and let it simmer
in the butter. Stir the flour smoothly, let
brown. Chop up tomatoes, parsley,
herbs and the rest, and add them
one and all to the browned flour and
onions. Season generously.
Add the shrimp (boiled and peeled)
and let them cook for twenty minutes
on a mild fire.
Take them off and put in Worcestershire. Your respect for shrimp will
shoot to zenith.

Jack Gill

# FRENCH FRIED SHRIMP

| | |
|---|---|
| 1 cup flour | 1 cup ice water |
| ½ Teaspoon sugar | 2 tablespoons melted fat |
| ½ teaspoon salt | or oil |
| 1 egg | 2 pounds fresh shrimp |

Combine ingredients, except shrimp; beat well. Peel shell from shrimp, leaving last section and tail intact. Cut through back to divide in half, but do not sever; remove black vein. Dip shrimp in batter; fry in deep fat 375° until golden brown. Drain on absorbent paper. Serve with tartar or soy sauce. Shrimp are much improved if allowed to stand in batter for several hours.

Mrs. Robert Q. Henry, Jr.

# SHRIMP AND RICE

| | |
|---|---|
| 1 can shrimp | 6 tablespoons tomato catsup |
| 1 pint cream | 6 drops tabasco |
| 2 cups cooked rice | 1 teaspoon Worcestershire |
| 1 tablespoon butter | |

Mix all. Place in casserole and bake in moderate oven 1 hour.

Edith Adkins

# DEVILED TUNA FISH

2 cups flaked tuna
1 cup evaporated milk
1½ teaspoon salt
¼ teaspoon pepper
1 tablespoon minced onion
3 chopped hard cooked eggs
2 teaspoons prepared mustard
¼ cup bread crumbs
1 tablespoon melted butter

Combine all ingredients except crumbs and butter. Pour into a well greased casserole. Sprinkle with crumbs mixed with butter. Bake 30 minutes, uncovered, in a 375° oven — until golden brown. Serves 4 generously.

Canned salmon or crab meat may be substituted for tuna. Don't forget you can make this hours ahead of time, putting it in oven just before serving.

Nancy M. Anthony

# TUNA FISH CASSEROLE

1 can white meat tuna
3 hard boiled eggs
grated yellow cheese
white sauce

## White Sauce

2 tablespoons butter
2 tablespoons flour
2 cups milk
2 tablespoons white wine
1/4 teaspoon paprika
salt to taste

Butter casserole. Peel hard boiled eggs and cut in half. Place in bottom of casserole. Put fish in colander and pour boiling water over to remove oil. Break fish over eggs carefully and cover with sauce; sprinkle with grated cheese and bake in moderate oven until browned.

Mrs. J. B. Powell

# MEATS

## PORK EN CASSEROLE

6 thick pork chops    1 teaspoon salt
4 large onions        1 teaspoon pepper
1 tablespoon pwd. sage 1 teaspoon curry powder
     1 heaping tablespoon flour

Cut up the onions and mix with sage. Mix together the flour, salt, pepper and curry powder. Dip the pork chops in this mixture.

Put the onions into a large casserole, lay the chops on top, cover with hot water and simmer for 2½ or 3 hours uncovered in moderate oven 325° or until very tender and brown.

            Mrs. Thomas T. Firth

## PORK AND SWEET POTATO CASSEROLE

3 cups diced cooked pork
2 cups diced cooked sweet potatoes
1 medium sized onion, grated
1 green pepper, chopped fine
1 cup white sauce or gravy

Combine ingredients. Add salt, pepper, celery salt to taste. Bake in moderate oven 350° for 30 minutes.

            Mrs. R. S. Jones

# CHOPS IN CASSEROLE

4 medium large lean pork chops
2 tablespoons olive oil
2 cups diced celery
2 cups or 1 medium can tomatoes
1 large onion
1 medium size green pepper
salt, pepper, flour

Put oil in hot skillet and brown chops well after having seasoned with salt and pepper. Either leave in skillet or remove to casserole. Cover with vegetables, adding more salt and pepper as required, add tomatoes last. Dust top with flour, to make little creamy when done, then enough water (about 1 cup) being careful not to disturb flour on top. Cover and bake at 350°, about 1 hour or until vegetables are tender. Add more water if necessary.

Mrs. Harry Clark, Sr.

# Pork Chops Baked in Sour Cream

4 loin pork chops cut ½ inch thick
½ cup water
1 bay leaf
2 tablespoons vinegar
1 tablespoon sugar
½ cup sour cream

Wipe chops with damp cloth. Season with salt and pepper, dredge with flour and brown in small amount of fat. Insert 1 clove in each chop and place in casserole. Add other ingredients, cover and bake in moderate oven (350°) about 1½ hours or until chops are done. Serves 4.

Mrs. H. V. L. Bloomfield

# HAM AND PORK LOAF

1 pound ground cured ham
1½ pound pork steak, ground
2 beaten eggs
1 cup milk
1 cup bread or cracker crumbs
Salt and pepper to taste

Mix all and pack in loaf pan and bake in 350° oven.

Cook for at least 5 minutes:
1½ cups brown sugar
2 tablespoons prepared mustard
½ cup vinegar
½ cup water

When the meat loaf begins to brown, pour on the syrup and cook about 2 hours, basting often.

Serve with horseradish sauce.

Nita Henry Nevius

# BAKED SLICE COUNTRY HAM

Cut slice from the middle of ham 1½ inch thick. Place in baking dish. Sprinkle with ¼ cup brown sugar, add 1 cup pineapple juice. Bake for 2 hours in 350° oven. Garnish with sliced pineapple before serving.

Mrs. Wyatt D. Pickering

# DRESSING FOR HAM

1 onion
1 pound pecan nuts
2 tablespoon mustard seed
3 large cucumber pickles

Chop fine and season with:

pepper
1 teaspoon allspice
1 teaspoon cloves
a very little salt

Combine and add 1 egg, mix thoroughly. Use as topping for ham slice or baked whole ham.

Mrs. Samuel T. Kennard

# FAVORITE SPARERIBS

| | |
|---|---|
| 4 pounds spareribs | 1 teaspoon salt |
| ½ cup flour | 1 teaspoon seasoning salt |
| 1 cup water | dash cayenne |

Sprinkle spareribs with salt, pepper and flour. Place in shallow pan. Brown in oven. Cook 1 hour slowly, adding water if needed.

## BARBECUE SAUCE

| | |
|---|---|
| 2 green peppers | ¼ teaspoon nutmeg |
| 2 onions | 1 cup chile sauce |
| ½ cup butter | 1 teaspoon Tabasco |
| 2 cup water | ½ teaspoon salt |
| 1 tablespoon flour | 1 clove garlic |
| 3 tablespoons Worcestershire | |

Melt butter in heavy pan. Add onions, garlic and peppers. Cook 10 minutes. Add seasonings. Cook five minutes more, pour over spare-ribs, simmer for 20 minutes.

Avis E. Johnson

# BARBECUED   SPARE RIBS

3 pounds   spare ribs
⅓ cup water                    ¾ cup  vinegar
⅓ cup butter                   ⅓ cup chili sauce
3 tablespoons Horseradish   ½ teaspoon  salt
3 tablespoons Worcestershire  sauce
dash of cayenne

Wipe spareribs and crack bones across.
Lay them on a broiler rack and broil
½ hour or until brown and crisp, basting
occasionally with a sauce made from all
the other ingredients mixed together.

Make a gravy with the sauce left over
with some of the drippings from spareribs.

Mrs. S.N. Hersloff

# HAM IN SHERRY

For ¾ inch of frying ham mix:

    2 tablespoons brown sugar
    ½ teaspoon ground cloves
    ½ teaspoon ground cinnamon

Rub mixture well into each side of ham. Place in frying pan over slow heat and cook until slightly browned on both sides.

Add 2 ounces sherry wine, cover tightly and cook over slow heat until done — about 10-15 minutes.

Southern spoon bread is a good complement to this dish.

            Mrs. Zebulon Stafford

# FRYING PAN STEW FOR BOATS

1 pound top round steak in ½ inch cubes
4 onions cut up          1 can giant peas
1 can tomato sauce      salt and pepper
     1 can small potatoes, halved

Brown meat and onions in ½ butter and ½ shortening. Sprinkle 2 heaping tablespoons flour over meat, stir, and make gravy with consomme or water. Add drained peas, potatoes, and tomato sauce. Season well and simmer until thoroughly heated. Serves 4 well.

Mrs. Carroll M. Elder

—:—:—:—:—:—:—:—:—:—

# PORK TENDERLOIN

Put large lump butter in skillet and brown tenderloin on both sides. Remove meat and thicken butter with a little flour. To this add: ½ green pepper chopped fine, ½ tablespoon Worcestershire, 2-3 tablespoons chili sauce, dash nutmeg.

Replace meat, add a little water, cover and simmer for 20 minutes. Add 1 small can mushrooms and juice. Cover and simmer slowly for 1 hour, basting occasionally.

Mrs. Alfred R. Roberts

## SOMERVILLE MEAT LOAF

2 pounds beef, ground
¾ cup suet
2 small onions
3 cups soft bread crumbs
3 teaspoons salt
4 tablespoons Worcestershire
2 eggs
4 tablespoons Horseradish
1 teaspoon dry mustard
4 tablespoons minced green pepper
¾ cup tomato catsup

Mix well all ingredients except the catsup.
Pack into greased bread pan. Cover top
with tomato catsup and bake for 45 minutes
at 400°.

This loaf may be made of left over meat if
desired and is delicious either hot or cold.

Katherine A. Fisher

# MEAT SOUFFLÉ

2 tablespoons butter
2 tablespoons flour
2 cups hot milk
½ cup stale bread crumbs
½ onion, chopped
2 cups ground meat (beef, lamb, veal)
2 eggs, separated

Make cream sauce of flour, butter and milk. Add bread crumbs, onion, and meat. Mix thoroughly, season, remove from fire and stir in beaten egg yolks. Pour into buttered baking dish, then fold in stiffly beaten egg whites.

Bake in 350° oven for 1 hour.

Mrs. J. Carter Richardson

— — - — — - — — - — — - — — - —

# BARBECUED BEEF TENDERLOIN

1 five pound beef tenderloin cut on the bias in slices 1½ - 2 inches thick. Brush with sauce made of vinegar, catsup, sugar, garlic, mustard, salt and pepper. Broil.

Mrs. Durrie B. Hardin

# CORNISH PASTIES

1 pound round steak or chuck
4 potatoes
2 onions
salt, pepper, Worcestershire to taste

Grind the above ingredients together.

A pie crust recipe using 3 cups of flour, 1 cup shortening, 1 teaspoon salt 6 tablespoons water makes pastry for above filling.

Roll round pieces of pastry dough to circles about 7 - 8 inches diameter. Place 1/3 - 1/2 cup filling on it, fold over, turn back edges and flute between fingers. Slit a few times to allow steam to escape. Bake 30 - 45 minutes in a hot oven. Excellent hot or cold.

Catharine C. Olds

## MEAT SOUFFLÉ
### (left over meat may be used)

| | |
|---|---|
| 2 cups scalded milk | 1 onion, chopped |
| 1 tablespoon butter | 2 tablespoon parsley |
| ¾ cup fine bread crumbs | 1 teaspoon salt |
| 3 egg yolks, beaten | 3 egg whites, beaten |
| 2 cups ground meat | |

Combine all ingredients except whites of eggs.
Mix well, then fold in egg whites. Bake in
moderate oven (350°) for 30 minutes.

Marie M. Riley

════════════════════════════════

## ROAST BEEF HASH
### (left over roast beef)

| | |
|---|---|
| 2 cups cubed beef (cooked) | dash of pepper |
| 6 medium potatoes (diced) | 1 teaspoon salt |
| 2 carrots (diced) | 1 large onion (sliced) |

Combine ingredients with gravy left from roast.
Add water enough to make 2 cups liquid.
Cook until potatoes are tender. Thicken as
desired.

Mrs. Russel Hallowell

# CHILI CON CARNE

1 cup thinly sliced onion
3 tablespoons fat or salad oil
1 #2 can tomatoes
1 #2 can kidney beans
3 tablespoons Chili powder
2 teaspoons sugar
½ teaspoon salt
½ teaspoon pepper
Dash Cayenne Pepper
4 garlic cloves
3 strips bacon, diced
2 lbs. ground beef

Saute onion in fat until tender.
Add tomatoes, kidney beans, Chili powder,
sugar, salt, pepper, Cayenne and garlic.
Simmer 30 minutes. Remove garlic. Fry
bacon until crisp; add meat. Cook,
stirring frequently until well browned.
Add meat to tomatoe mixture. Serves 8.

Mrs. P. N. Horne

# CREOLE MEAT BALLS

2 cups tomato sauce
1 large chopped onion or
1 small chopped clove garlic
1 green pepper chopped
1 bay leaf - salt - pepper
¼ teaspoon thyme
4 tablespoons olive oil
1 pound ground beef

Make meat into balls, seasoning with salt and pepper. Brown in skillet, and remove. Put oil, onion or garlic, green pepper into skillet and brown slowly. Add tomato sauce and seasonings. Bring to a boil, lower heat, add meat balls and cover. Simmer for at least 1 hour. Add hot water if sauce becomes too thick. Serve over fluffy rice.

Emily W. Pugh

# KIDNEYS IN CLARET

Slice veal kidneys quite thin. Melt butter in frying pan, add 1 thinly sliced onion. When butter is brown, drop in the kidneys, add salt and pepper. Cook through, but not too long. Remove kidneys add flour to butter and brown. Add 1 cup or more claret. Put kidneys back in sauce and serve.

Carroll M. Elder

# Jacob's Kidney Stew

1 large beef kidney
4 medium potatoes
1 grated onion
butter, salt and pepper

Take large kidney, cut out fat. Cook in a large amount of water and when half done change the water. When tender, dice kidney and potatoes. Put kidney into the potato water and thicken. Add seasoning to taste.

Mrs. R. S. Jones

# KIDNEY STEW

1 large kidney
1 onion
1 1/2 tablespoons butter
1 1/4 tablespoons flour
2 tablespoons Sherry
Salt and pepper

Remove fat and sinews from kidney. Wash well and put in saucepan with salted water to cover. Allow to come to a boil, and simmer for 5 minutes or until tender. Remove kidney and cut into small pieces, keeping water.

Slice onion and cook with butter in frying pan. When light brown, stir in flour and 1 1/4 cup water in which kidney was boiled. Add sherry and kidney. Season to taste.

Mrs. Richard MacSherry

# MEAT AND MACARONI

1/2 pound ground beef  
1 small onion chopped  
1 1/2 cups tomato juice  
2 tablespoons green pepper  
2 tablespoons shortening  

1 cup catsup  
1 cup macaroni  
1 teaspoon salt  
pepper  

Melt shortening, brown meat, onion and green pepper. Add seasonings, tomato juice, catsup and macaroni. Cover and bring to a boil, then cook over low heat for 1 hour.

Mrs. Raymond O. Dean

\\\ /// \\\ /// \\\ /// \\\ /// \\\ /// \\\ /// \\\ /// \\\ /// \\\ /// \\\

# BAKED MACARONI AND CHIPPED BEEF

Cover 1/4 pound chipped beef with hot water and let stand 10 minutes. Drain. Arrange in buttered baking dish alternate layers cooked macaroni and chipped beef — 2 layers of each. Pour 2 cups white sauce over all, top with buttered bread crumbs. Bake in hot oven until crumbs are brown.

Mrs. Thurston Harrison

## CHIPPED BEEF A LA KING

½ pound of dried beef
1 cup mushrooms, sliced
1 green pepper, chopped
1 pimento, chopped
½ cup butter
2 tablespoons flour
2 cups rich milk
¼ cup of sherry
salt and pepper

Place half of butter in saucepan and heat the mushrooms, peppers and pimento until soft. Place beef in a little cold water and let stand for half an hour. Squeeze beef dry. Pull into small pieces. Melt half of butter in double boiler and add beef, stirring occasionally until cooked. Add flour, sprinkling it over meat. Stir until absorbed by butter. Add milk slowly and bring to a boil, stirring constantly. Reduce heat and simmer 10 minutes. Add cooked mushrooms and mixture, stirring until well blended. Remove from fire and add sherry. Stir it through the mixture. Add salt and pepper depending on saltiness of beef. Serve with wild rice.

Serves four.

Kitty Parker Rouse

Leg of lamb "à la venison"

Lard the lamb and wrap
in a cloth soaked (but not wrung
out) in vinegar. Let stand at
least 24 hours.

Unwrap and roast as
usual, basting. Let gravy get
very brown. (Do not use
flour.) Add sour cream.

Mrs. Frank Gregson —

# LAMB CURRY with RICE

2 pounds boned lamb shoulder
1 tablespoon fat
1 sliced onion
1 teaspoon salt
⅛ teaspoon pepper
1 or more teaspoon curry powder
1 tablespoon flour
2 cups boiling water
1 sliced apple
4 cups cooked rice
Chutney sauce

Trim the fat from lamb and cut into 1½ inch cubes. Brown in the fat in a heavy skillet with onion. Add the salt, curry powder, flour and pepper and stir well.

Add the sliced apple and boiling water, cover and simmer slowly, stirring occasionally until tender — 1 - 1½ hours. Arrange on a hot platter and surround with cooked rice. Serve with chutney sauce.

Mrs. Robert G. Henry, Jr.

# VEAL CASSEROLE "MACSHERRY"

1 large veal cutlet or 4 veal chops cut 1½" thick
(flour on both sides)

4 medium carrots
½ cup cream
½ teaspoon thyme
1 teaspoon Kitchen Bouquet
¼ cup Sherry

2 medium onions
1 teaspoon marjoram
1 bay leaf
2 tablespoons flour
salt and pepper to taste.

Scrape and cut carrots in small pieces. Chop onions. Combine and boil in 1 cup water until done. Drain and save vegetable water.

Cut meat in serving pieces and brown well in 3 tablespoons Crisco, in iron frying pan. Remove to bottom of greased casserole with carrots and onions on top. Add bay leaf.

Put flour, marjoram and thyme in frying pan with 2 tablespoons fat and smooth to a paste. Add cream and vegetable juice slowly, then blend in Kitchen Bouquet. Pour over meat and vegetables. Add sherry.

Cook at 350° for 45 minutes.

It is better served second or third day.

Mrs. Richard MacSherry

# HUNGARIAN SUPPER

2 pounds lean veal
½ cup butter
4 large onions
1 clove garlic
1 can tomatoes (fresh may be used)
1 heaping teaspoon salt
½ Teaspoon freshly ground black pepper
1 Teaspoon paprika
1 Teaspoon grated nutmeg
½ Teaspoon mace
1 Tablespoon sugar
1 cup sour cream

Cut veal in Two inch cubes and sear on all sides in melted butter. Add sliced onions and chopped garlic and cook until yellow. Add Tomatoes and seasonings. Simmer until veal is Tender and sauce boils down— about 2½ hours.

About 15 mins. before serving add sour cream. Serve with fluffy rice, noodles or. macaroni.

Mrs. George D. Olds

# VEAL CUTLETS – FRENCH STYLE

Pound 2 veal cutlets with flour and salt and pepper. Brown in butter with 2 finely chopped onions and 1 tomato. Add 1 cup sour cream, ¼ pound mushrooms and simmer until done.

Catharine C. Olds

# VEAL PAPRIKA

1 pound veal sliced thin
1 teaspoon onion chopped fine
4 slices bacon          ¼ teaspoon salt
1 teaspoon paprika      1 cup sour cream
1 cup tomato sauce

Brown bacon in iron skillet. Cut veal into servings and brown in bacon fat. Brown onions, add sour cream, tomato sauce, salt and paprika. Cover and simmer about 20 minutes.

Mrs. Gibson Graham

# PAPRIKA SNITZEL

2 pounds cubed veal
1 pound of onions chopped and fried
⅛ pound butter
2 tablespoon paperika
1 pint sour cream

Brown the cubed veal and season with salt and pepper. When this is thoroughly cooked, add the onions and simmer for one hour longer. When ready to serve add sour cream. Serve this over boiled noodles.

Rebecca M. Jefferson

"Anything that grows below the earth must be planted on the wane of the moon, and what grows above the ground must be planted on the increase of the moon."

# RABBIT

Soak rabbit in cold salted water for ½ hour. Cut in serving pieces, flour, salt, and pepper each piece, brown quickly in dutch oven. Add 2 medium sliced onions, one small hot red pepper, whole, and cover with hot water. Put cover on immediately, turn flame very low and let simmer 1½ hours. More water may be added if needed. Before serving, add small amount of thickening to gravy.

Muskrat can be cooked this way, but should be soaked in salted water over night.

Mrs. Robert F. Austin

# FROGS LEGS IN RED WINE

Fry some minced parsley and onion lightly in butter. Put in the frogs, lightly floured and seasoned with salt and pepper. Cook quickly for a few minutes. Reduce flame and add equal parts chicken stock (canned) and red wine — amount depending on number of frogs. When frogs are tender, remove and if too much liquid remains, reduce over brisk flame.

Carroll M. Elder

## RABBIT EN CASSEROLE

| | |
|---|---|
| 2 rabbits | 2 cups hot water |
| 2 sliced onions | 1 cup cold water |
| 2 celery stalks | 12 stoned olives |
| 1 cup chopped carrots | 1 tablespoon capers |
| 1 bay leaf     1 tablespoon | Worcestershire |
| 2 heaping tablespoons butter | 2 tablespoons lard |
| 2 heaping tablespoons flour | salt and pepper |

Skin and joint the rabbits; then put them into a casserole. Add onions, celery, carrots, bay leaf, shortening and cold water.
Simmer for 30 minutes, then remove rabbits. Add butter and flour to the pan. Stir over fire until brown; then add hot water, stirring until smooth.
Add salt, sauce, capers, olives, pepper and the rabbits. Cover closely and bake for 40 minutes.

Mrs. Thomas T. Firth

# CURRIED RABBIT or MUSKRAT

Cut meat in serving pieces and soak in strong salt water for several hours. Dry, dredge with flour, salt and pepper and brown in either bacon or salt pork fat. Put meat in covered sauce pan with a little water to steam.

Mix 2 teaspoons curry powder, 1 teaspoon sugar and 1 heaping tablespoon flour. Meanwhile put 1 large sliced onion into fat left in skillet. Add curry mixture to onion and brown together.

Add slowly: 1 pint water, 1 cup strained tomatoes, small handful raisins and 1 cup chopped sour apple. Cook until smooth and pour over rabbit and continue cooking until meat is very tender. When ready to serve add 1 cup hot milk. Pour rabbit on platter and surround with hot cooked rice.

Mrs. Joseph A. Ross

# BELGIAN HARE À LA MARYLAND

1 rabbit, cut in portions
1 cup flour
2 eggs, beaten
cracker crumbs
4 tablespoons melted butter
1 small onion, minced
2 bay leaves
Salt and pepper
hot water

Wash pieces of rabbit, wipe dry. Sprinkle with salt and pepper and roll each piece in flour, beaten egg and cracker crumbs. Brown in roaster in which butter was melted, add onion and bay leaves; cover. Roast for 1½ hours in moderate oven - 350° - 375°, basting with 1-2 cups hot water, depending upon amount of gravy desired. Remove cover, and continue to roast for 30 minutes, basting frequently.

Mrs. Robert C. Morris

# MUSKRAT TRED AVON

Cut up 3 muskrats, place in crock or enamel pan and cover with the following marinade :

6 sprigs parsley } bruised well
6 celery tops

1 carrot , 1 onion , 1 leek , 1 clove garlic
        all sliced fine

6 pepper corns          2 bay leaves

2 tablespoons olive oil    pinch cayenne
enough red wine to cover meat

Leave in marinade about 12 hours stirring 3 or 4 times.

Take meat out, season, roll in flour and fry in ½ butter and ½ lard until brown and crisp.

Meanwhile cook marinade until vegetables are tender, strain and use juice to make gravy.

Just before serving, add 1 teaspoon currant jelly to gravy.

Mrs. Carroll Elder

# WILD DUCKS

Maryland hunters divide ducks into two groups: those you eat, and Trash ducks. You eat Trash ducks too, but there is some difference in the cooking process.

Canvas back, red head, and black duck are drawn, wiped clean or washed quickly in very little water, and dried. The oven must be very hot, to sear the duck inside and out. No stuffing should interfere with this searing process. Place in low sided oven dish and cook 20 - 25 minutes at 450°. The meat should be flesh red, not blue.

Trash ducks are sometimes soaked for a few hours in salted water to remove the strong-tasting blood, then wiped dry. An onion or ½ orange is put inside to absorb the fishy taste of the fish eating varieties.

Coot, according to some authorities, are nailed on a hickory board, put in a deep pan, boiled for 4-5 hours, then discarded. The board is said to have a fine, high flavor, though scarcely tender!

# STUFFED MALLARD DUCK

1 mallard duck
1 quart bread crumbs
1 tablespoon minced onion
1 teaspoon salt
1 teaspoon sage
½ teaspoon pepper
1 egg
½ cup warm water
2 tablespoons sausage drippings or butter

Singe, draw and wipe out mallard duck. Stuff with combined ingredients, tie wings and legs down to sides with twine. Bake in a hot oven from 30 to 40 minutes. Baste frequently with fat from pan.

Mrs. William B. Davis

# PANNED PARTRIDGES A LA TALBOT

Split birds down back; place in open pan with four tablespoons melted butter, a little bit of water, salt, pepper, celery stalk and parsley. Cook in hot oven for ten minutes, constantly turning and basting the birds so as to brown them evenly; then cover the pan tightly and cook ten minutes longer. Remove from oven, garnish with parsley and serve on toast. Nice served with a fruit salad.

Mrs. L. H. Chaffinch

## SQUIRREL

Cut in sections as rabbit. Dredge in flour with salt and pepper added to taste. Brown in bacon fat. Add a little water, cover and steam 1½ hours or until tender.

Mrs. M. Mae Pahlman

# DOVE

Clean and split doves down the back, and open flat. Salt and pepper both sides thoroughly.

Place flat in a large iron frying pan with 1/8 inch butter and brown on both sides over hot flame with cover on for 10 minutes.

Add 1 wineglass of red wine while pan is very hot, recover immediately and place in 250° oven for 10-20 minutes.

Serve with red wine and loaf of French bread crisped in the oven while doves are cooking.

Donald S. Ross

# PLANTATION SQUABS

Have squabs split down the back. Place 2 tablespoons of butter for each squab in a heavy iron frying pan and when the butter is hot, sear the squabs on both sides.

Turn the birds cut side down, cover the pot, and continue to cook. Turn the birds and cook the other side.

Sprinkle salt and pepper on the squabs and add 1 cup of boiling water. Cover and steam a while longer. The entire cooking time is about 20 minutes.

Mrs. S. N. Hersloff

# PARTRIDGE, HUNTER'S STYLE

1 partridge        1 cup chopped cabbage
2 small carrots diced    1 onion, diced
    3 to 4 large cabbage leaves
   3 slices of bacon, sautéed and crumbled

Clean bird and stuff with a mixture of chopped cabbage and bacon. Wrap securely in cabbage leaves. Place in a pan with 1 inch of boiling water in it, add the carrots and onion. Let simmer, covered, for 1½ hours.

Mrs. S. N. Hersloff

## _PARTRIDGE _.

Birds should hang for
several days to improve flavor.
Clean, soak in salt water. Rub inside and out with salt, pepper, and
thyme to taste. Roast for 30 minutes
in hot oven.

## _WOODCOCK _

Like most game, these birds should
hang for several days. Wrap in
larding pork and roast for 10 minutes
in hot oven. Serve on toast with
gravy made of the pan juices.

## ROAST PHEASANT

Sprinkle with salt, pepper to taste, and rub well with butter. Cover with thin sheet of larding pork. Roast in a moderate oven for about 40 minutes, or until done. Serve with juices in the pan, partially free from fat and strained. Accompany with wild rice and tart jelly.

## CANADIAN GOOSE

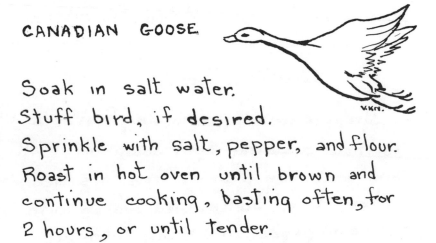

Soak in salt water.
Stuff bird, if desired.
Sprinkle with salt, pepper, and flour.
Roast in hot oven until brown and continue cooking, basting often, for 2 hours, or until tender.

## Roast Venison

3-4 lbs. roast
Sprinkle 2 Tsp. salt with a little pepper.
Dredge with flour.
Place in an iron pan with 2 tbsp. fat.
Sear on all sides until brown. Add a
small amount of water, cover pan
and turn heat low. Add a little water
when it seems dry. Cook until tender
<u>very slowly</u>. Remove from pan and
This makes delicious gravy.

Helen B. Adams

---

## Quail on Toast

Dress carefully, removing feathers
without scalding. Split down the back
and soak for a short Time in salted
water. Dry, butter well, season with
salt and pepper and broil, Turning
frequently, until done. Serve bird,
breast side up, on buttered Toast and
garnish with currant jelly.

Mrs William B. Davis

## SOUTHERN FRIED CHICKEN #1

Select 2 pound fryer. Draw and disjoint. Dredge each piece in flour, salt and pepper to taste. Fry in hot fat until golden brown on each side, then lower flame, cover tightly and let steam until tender. Serve on hot platter, garnished with slices of lemon.

Mrs. H. A. Beach

## FRIED CHICKEN #2

Make batter of 1 whole egg, ½ cup flour, salt and pepper. Coat disjointed fryer with batter, fry until golden in ½ butter and ½ shortening. Cover and cook until tender. Remove cover for last few minutes to crisp chicken. Be sure to cook very slowly.

Transfer chicken to hot platter, add rounded tablespoon flour to fat in pan, add 1 cup milk or cream, cook till thickened.

Mrs. Charles E. Wheeler

# CHICKEN À LA TARTARE

1 broiling chicken
¼ pound melted butter
4 sprigs parsley
2 scallions or 1 onion
¼ pound mushrooms
¼ clove garlic
bread crumbs
salt and pepper

Place chicken in frying pan in which butter has been melted. Chop parsley, onion, mushrooms and garlic. Add to the butter with a seasoning of salt and pepper. Cover pan and allow chicken to simmer gently for about 15 minutes, turning occasionally to absorb the flavor of seasonings.

Remove chicken, roll in fine bread crumbs and broil until well browned. Serve with the butter sauce.

The pre-cooking prevents "underdoneness" of the broiler

Mrs. Thomas Hughes

# DEVILED CHICKEN LEGS

Chicken legs
English mustard
prepared mustard
bread crumbs
9 tablespoons butter
2 egg yolks
1 teaspoon sugar
2 tablespoons vinegar
salt and pepper

Remove skin from legs and spread with thin paste of English mustard and cold water. Roll legs in fine bread crumbs, salt and pepper and place large lump of butter on each. Place in pre-heated moderate broiler and broil for 30 minutes, turning often so they are golden brown.

Meanwhile prepare mustard sauce. To egg yolks add 2 tablespoons cold water, 6 tablespoons butter, salt, pepper, sugar, and vinegar. Cook slowly in double boiler, beating constantly. When foaming add 1 teaspoon prepared mustard and 1 tablespoon English mustard. Cook slowly for 10 minutes until light and foamy. Add 1 tablespoon butter

Mrs. C.F. Houston Miller

# Chicken "Champs Isles"

3 pounds spinach or broccoli
1 Tablespoon butter
1 garlic bud
salt and pepper
1 pinch marjoram
1 pinch basil
1 tablespoon flour
⅓ cup heavy cream

Cook spinach, drain well, chop fine
Brown butter, add seasonings, blend
in flour. Add cream.

| | |
|---|---|
| 1 chicken (cooked) | ¾ cup chicken stock |
| 3 Tablespoons butter | salt and pepper |
| 3 tablespoon flour | 6 thin slices of |
| ¾ cup cream | Canadian bacon, frizzled |
| 1 cup grated cheese | |

Add spinach to the cream sauce and
cook 5 minutes, stirring constantly. Put
a layer of spinach about 1½ inch thick
in a casserole. Place good sized pieces
of chicken on spinach. Make a cream
sauce of butter, flour, chicken stock, and
cream, adding the cut-up pieces of
bacon to it. Spoon sauce over the
chicken.
Sprinkle cheese on top. Heat in the
oven. Serves 6

Mrs. Frank Gregson

# CHICKEN AND DUMPLINGS

4 pound chicken, cut up
2 small carrots, sliced
3 sweet potatoes, cut
3 Irish potatoes, cut
Whole small onions

Put chicken in large pot, add salt, cover well with water and cook until nearly done. Add vegetables and continue cooking until vegetables are nearly done.

Dumplings :

2 cups flour          ½ teaspoon salt
1 teaspoon baking powder
4 tablespoon chicken fat
enough water to mix for rolling

Divide dough in 3 parts. Roll 2 parts, cut in squares, add 1 part to simmering chicken, and cook 5 minutes. Add 2nd part and cook 5 minutes more. The 3rd part can be added as dumplings or used as top crust.

Mrs. Wyatt D. Pickering

# STEWED CHICKEN SUPREME

2 cups Sauterne wine
2 cups water
1½ teaspoons salt
1 small onion, chopped
chopped parsley
2 stalks celery chopped
4 - 5 pound chicken
4 tablespoons flour
½ cup cream
2 egg yolks beaten
1 cup cooked peas

Heat water and 1 cup wine to boiling point in large kettle. Add salt, onion, parsley and celery and cut up chicken. Cover and simmer until tender.

Remove chicken. Add remaining wine and enough water to make 3 cups liquid. Thicken with flour mixed with cream and egg yolks. Add peas and serve over hot chicken.

Mrs. Gibson Graham

# CHICKEN CACCIATORE

1 stewing chicken, cut up
1 clove garlic
3 tbl. of olive oil
2 onions
1 6 ounce can tomato paste
1 quart canned tomatoes
½ pound thin spaghetti
thyme, salt, pepper, and flour

In heavy frying pan or iron pot, brown clove of garlic in olive oil and remove it. Brown chicken, which has been floured, in olive oil and set aside. Add onions, finely chopped, and cook until transparent. Add tomato paste, pinch of thyme, salt and pepper and canned tomatoes. Simmer until well blended, then add chicken and cook slowly until chicken is done. Just before serving remove chicken to hot platter and mix sauce with ½ pound just-cooked thin spaghetti.

This dish is even better the day after it is made.

Sauce may also include tiny meat balls or cut mushrooms.

Mrs. George D. Olds III

# CHICKEN PAPRIKA

1 cup cooking oil (Olive oil)
6 onions sliced
1 medium can tomatoes
6-8 pieces young chicken
3 pinches herbs - basil, marjoram,
  and rosemary
Salt and pepper to taste
½ cup heavy sour cream
6 teaspoons Hungarian paprika

Place cooking oil in deep heavy skillet (Olive oil makes superior flavor). Brown onions gently, add chicken and brown on both sides. Cook through, sprinkle lightly with flour. Add tomatoes and all the seasonings, and simmer ½ - ¾ hour.

Remove chicken to platter and add sour cream to sauce left in skillet. Mix and stir swiftly until very hot and thick, and pour over chicken. Garnish with chopped parsley.

Mrs. C. D. Cox

## ARROZ CON POLLO
## (CHICKEN IN RICE)

2 cups rice
1 can pimentoes
2 bay leaves
4 tablespoons olive oil
3 large onions chopped fine
3 large tomatoes chopped fine
5 pounds chicken, cut up
1 cup white wine
1 can petit pois or 1 package frozen peas cooked
3 smoked sausages, cut up
1 package frozen shrimps
1 can hearts of artichokes (optional)

1 bottle olives
1 teas. saffron
1 teaspoon salt
½ teaspoon black pepper

Into iron dutch oven put oil; heat, add onions and brown, add tomatoes and simmer 10 minutes, then add bay leaves, salt, pepper, white wine, chicken and a little water if necessary. Cook until chicken is almost done, remove and add well washed rice; to liquid in dutch oven add 1 cup boiling water. (add more water to cook rice if needed) Take safron, place on paper and heat. When warm, crumble and put into a cup with ½ cup boiling water. Stir, strain off liquid; add to pot in which rice is cooking. When rice is almost done, add chicken, peas, shrimp, olives, sausage, artichokes. Place in a casserole, placing pimentoes on top. Cover with brown paper well greased, keeping in warm oven till ready to serve.

Mrs. Alfred Lacazette

## Country Captain

3 chickens, cut in pieces the size you wish
flour
2 green peppers, chopped
6 onions, chopped.
1 large can tomatoes
1/2 pound almonds, blanched
1 small can pimentoes, cut in small pieces
1 bunch celery, chopped.
1/2 pound mushrooms
orange juice or wine to t███████
cayenne

Wash chicken in salt water and dry. Roll in flour and saute in frying pan until brown. Then put in roasting pan, cover with water and put in all other ingredients. Allow to simmer very slowly until chicken is tender. The chicken can be boned then or served as is. Serve with rice.

The ingredients may be varied according to taste. Different vegtables can be added. Both orange juice and wine can be used.

Mrs. Howe Lagarde

# CHICKEN PANCAKES

2 cups flour          1½ cups milk
½ teaspoon salt      3 eggs

Sift flour and salt, add beaten eggs and milk. Beat until like thick cream. Grease #5 pan slightly and add just enough batter to cover pan thinly, and cook one side only. Turn pancakes on brown paper cooked side up.

## Chicken filling:

3 cups cooked chicken     1½ cups stock
½ cup green pepper        ½ cup onions
2 tablespoons chili sauce  1 teaspoon salt
3 tablespoons butter      3 tablespoons flour
½ cup mushrooms

Cut chicken, onions, green pepper and mushrooms in small cubes. Brown in butter slightly, add flour and seasonings. Mix well, add stock, and cook ½ hour. Let cool. Fill pancakes using 3 teaspoons chicken mixture to each cake. Roll and place in a well buttered pan. Bake in 400° oven about 25 minutes or until golden brown.

Serve with gravy made from chicken stock. Cooked turkey, veal or pork may be used in place of chicken.

Avis E. Johnson

# CHICKEN TETTRAZINI

2 cups finely shredded chicken
1/4 pound fresh mushrooms
3 tablespoons butter
1/2 pound thin spaghetti
salt

## CREAM SAUCE

2 tablespoons butter     2 cups chicken broth
2 tablespoons flour      1/2 cup heavy cream
2 tablespoons sherry

Thinly slice fresh mushrooms and sauté in the 3 tablespoons butter until soft and brown.

Break spaghetti into small pieces and cook in salted water until tender.

Make the cream sauce using butter and flour, gradually adding hot chicken broth, stirring until smooth and boiling point is reached, then stir in the cream and the sherry.

Divide sauce, add the shredded chicken to one half, the cooked spaghetti and mushrooms to the other half. Put spaghetti half into greased baking dish making a hole in the center for chicken mixture. Cover with Parmesian cheese and bake in 400° oven until lightly browned, about 10 minutes.

Mrs. Edward T. Bromfield

# CHICKEN LOAF

3 cups cooked chicken
1 cup soft bread crumbs
2 beaten eggs
½ teaspoon salt
¼ teaspoon paprika
¼ cup chopped pimiento
2 cups milk
½ cup cooked peas

Combine all ingredients and bake in slow oven 325° for 40 minutes. Serve mushroom sauce with this.

Mrs. Howard Bloomfield

# CHICKEN PIE

Cut up a 3 pound chicken, add salt to season and water to cover and boil until tender. Add 2 tablespoons butter and flour paste to thicken.

Line casserole with biscuit dough, bake 10 minutes in hot oven, add hot chicken mixture, top with crust and bake 10 minutes or until brown.

Mrs. Douglas Hanks

# CASSEROLE CHICKEN PIE

Disjoint a well cleaned chicken and simmer until tender in salted water. Remove chicken from broth and take meat from bones. Thicken the broth to consistency of thin gravy and return chicken meat to gravy.

Place in casserole and have little biscuits made from biscuit dough ready. See that biscuits are not more than ½ inch thick. Place biscuits on top of chicken in the casserole, and bake in 450° oven about 10 - 12 minutes.

Prepared biscuit mix is a good substitute for biscuit dough made at the time.

Mrs. Charles B. Adams

# CHICKEN CROQUETTES

5 pounds ground meat (chicken or veal)
1 pint cream and 1 pint milk
⅛ pound butter
1 cup bread crumbs
Salt and pepper

Let milk, cream and butter come to a boil, then mix in the bread crumbs. Stir in the ground meat, season with salt and pepper to taste.

Cool, mold into shape desired, roll in cracker crumbs, dip in beaten egg, roll in crumbs again, and fry in hot deep fat.

Mrs. Joseph A. Ross

# CHICKEN À LA KING

Prepare 1 cup very thick cream sauce
1 cup mushrooms
1 1/2 cups cubed chicken
salt and paprika
chicken stock
pimento, finely chopped
2 tablespoons lemon juice

Sauté mushrooms in butter, and add
to cream sauce. Dilute sauce with
the chicken stock, add the chicken
and other ingredients.

Shortly before serving, add the lemon
juice.

Serve on hot toast, in patty shells,
or on rice.

Nancy A. Schuyler

# CHICKEN CURRY #1

2 cups cold chicken
2 tablespoon butter
2 tablespoon flour
2 cups milk
1 tablespoon curry powder
salt, pepper, parsley

Cut chicken in small pieces. Melt butter, add flour and when blended, gradually add hot milk and seasonings. Stir over low fire until thick and add chicken.

Serve with boiled rice, garnish with raw bananas cut lengthwise, and top with parsley.

Chutney is especially good with this dish. Cold lamb or veal may be substituted for the chicken.

Mrs. Gardner Hazen

# CURRIED CHICKEN # 2

1 stewing chicken
3 tablespoons butter
2 tablespoons preserved ginger
1 cup onion, thinly sliced
1 large or 2 small limes
milk from 1 fresh cocoanut
½ teaspoon salt
4 whole cloves
1 teaspoon chopped fresh mint
⅛ teaspoon black pepper
3 teaspoons Indian curry powder
½ cup top milk
2 tablespoons cream

Cut up chicken and shake in a paper bag containing flour, salt and pepper.

Heat butter in heavy pan, add chopped ginger and onion. Add the chicken and brown until onion is golden. Add juice of lime, ½ cup water, milk from cocoanut and remaining seasonings. Cover and simmer ½ hour. Then add top milk, simmer until tender — ½ hour or more. Stir in cream before serving.

Serve with fluffy boiled rice, and have grated fresh cocoanut and chutney as side dishes.

Mrs. George D. Olds III

# OVEN FRIED CHICKEN

½ cup flour
½ cup fat
2 teaspoons salt
1 tablespoon paprika
pepper

Halve 2 pound broilers or cut 3 pound chicken in serving pieces. Blend flour, fat, seasonings. Spread this coating over chicken. Bake in shallow pan in moderate oven - 325° until tender, about an hour.

Mrs. D. C. Kirby, Jr.

---

# SAVORY DUCK

1 roasting duck
1 cup white wine
salt and pepper
1 cup water

Cut duck in serving pieces. Roll in seasoned flour and brown in hot fat. Place duck in pot, add wine and water, cover tightly, and simmer until tender. Remove duck, skim excess fat from liquid, and thicken gravy. Serve with fluffy rice.

Mrs. Gibson Graham

# TURKEY a la KING

2 cups milk
4 tablespoons flour
2 tablespoons butter or margarine
salt and pepper
2 cups of diced left over turkey
1 cup gravy
1 cup peas
1 diced pimento

Melt the butter and add flour stirring it
well. Add the milk, salt and pepper and cook
until the mixture starts to thicken. To this add
1 cup of warmed gravy and mix in well. Then
add the turkey, peas and the pimento. Cook
until the desired thickness is reached.
Serve hot on toast or waffles.

Mrs. Paul Dietrich

# TURKEY CROQUETTES

½ pound cooked Turkey
½ pound cooked ham
4 large mushrooms
1 cup consommé
1 egg yolk
bread crumbs
parsley, salt and pepper

Peel and chop mushrooms fine, sauté in butter. Slowly add consommé and cook down to half original quantity. Add parsley, salt and pepper, simmer for 10 minutes. Add egg yolk and pour mixture over meat. Cool. The consistency should be stiff enough to shape into croquettes, or into mock cutlets with a piece of macaroni for the bone. Dip in egg, bread crumbs, again in egg, then crumbs. Fry in hot fat.

Mrs. C. F. Huston Miller

"Eat a chicken gizzard to be pretty."

# GUINEA CASSEROLE

Cut up one quinea (stewing) into portions and sprinkle with salt and pepper.

Put into a large skillet and saute, these:

    3 tablespoons olive oil

    1 small clove of garlic

    1 medium onion, chopped fine

Remove the onion and garlic, discarding the latter. Brown the quinea in the hot oil, being careful not to burn.

Put the quinea in a casserole. Make a thin sauce in the skillet by adding ½ cup of sherry, flour, and the onion already cooked. Season quite highly with pepper, salt and cayenne.

Pour over the quinea in the casserole, cover, and bake slowly for 1½ to 2 hours.

Mr. Donald Ross

# EGGS IN NESTS

For each serving
1 slice bread, toasted on one side
1 slice cheese
1 egg
1 slice bacon

Butter the untoasted side of bread and top with the slice of cheese. Place on a buttered baking sheet.

Beat the egg white until peaks form. Arrange on the cheese in a circle with a hollow in the center. Slip the egg yolk into the hollow, dot with butter, sprinkle with salt and pepper. Bake in a moderate oven until egg yolk is set, garnish with crisp bacon and serve hot.

Mrs. Robert Cox

"Whistling girls and crowing hens
Always come to some bad end."

## EGGS BAKED IN TOMATOES

Remove the pulp from tomatoes and invert the skins to drain. Break into each cup one egg; dot with butter, sprinkle with salt and pepper; and bake in a moderate oven until the eggs are firm.

Mrs. H. V. L. Bloomfield.

"Always set a hen on an odd number of eggs. If you want cocks, put your eggs under the hen at ebb-tide. If you want pullets, place the eggs at high tide."

# EGGS FLORENTINE

1 tablespoon butter
1 teaspoon minced onion
1 teaspoon minced green pepper
8 tablespoons cooked sieved spinich
4 eggs salt and pepper to taste

Medium white sauce made with:
1 tablespoon butter
1 tablespoon flour
3/4 cup milk or cream
salt and pepper

2 tablespoons grated cheese

Saute the onions and green pepper in the butter for a few minutes and then add the spinach.

Butter four custard cups and divide the spinach mixture among them. Break an egg into each cup making a nest for them with a spoon. Cover with cream sauce, sprinkle with grated cheese, and bake until eggs are set.
This recipe may be made in a casserole dish instead of individual cups

Mrs. Howard Bloomfield

# SUNDAY NIGHT CHEESE

6 1/4 inch slices dry bread
2 tablespoons butter or margarine
1 teaspoon salt
1 teaspoon mustard
1 teaspoon worcestershire sauce
2 eggs slightly beaten
1 1/2 cups milk
2 cups grated cheese (1/2 pound)

Butter bread, line casserole with slices butter side down. Mix dry ingredients, add eggs, milk and cheese, stirring well. Pour mixture over bread, bake in moderate oven 350° for 30 minutes. Serve at once.

C. B. Cox

# CHEESE PUDDING

4 slices bread
3 cups milk
1 teaspoon salt
dash red pepper

3 eggs
1 1/2 cups cheese
1/4 teaspoon mustard

Butter bread cut in small squares. Line baking dish with bread, cover with cheese and layer of bread. Mix other ingredients with beaten eggs. Pour over cheese and bread, let stand 10 minutes. Bake in moderate oven 25 to 30 minutes.

Mrs. Raymond O. Yean

# FRENCH TOASTED SANDWICHES

6 slices Cheddar cheese
12 slices bread
3 eggs
½ teaspoon salt
1 cup milk

Beat eggs with fork, add milk and salt. Dip one side of slice of bread in mixture, place dipped side down in frying pan in which you have heated 2 tablespoons butter or fat. Top slice of bread with slice of cheese and cover with second bread slice, dipped side up.

Brown, turn whole sandwich and brown other side. The cheese will melt while bread browns. Add more butter to the pan as other sandwiches are cooked.

Serve hot with maple syrup.

Betty Jean Wheeler

# ITALIAN TOAST

1 pound cheese
2 eggs well beaten
1 cup milk or cream
1 teaspoon mustard
½ teaspoon salt
pepper
Breakfast bacon

Beat the eggs and add grated cheese, then the milk and other ingredients. Pour it over slices of bread on a baking sheet, and bake until it has fluffed up and browned. Serve immediately, garnished with crisp bacon.

This recipe is enough for 16 slices.

Miss Martha Goldsborough

# WELSH RAREBIT

½ pound sharp cheese
1 tablespoon butter
1 egg
1 dash red pepper or Tobasco
1 teaspoon mustard sauce
½ teaspoon salt
⅔ cup milk or cream

Dice cheese, add butter and the seasonings and part of the milk. Melt slowly over low flame, stirring constantly.

When smooth add yolk of egg beaten with remainder of milk, and stir until smooth. Take from fire and add stiffly beaten egg white. Let stand a few seconds and serve on toasted crackers.

Mrs. William T. Hammond

# WELSH RAREBIT WITH BEER

1 tablespoon butter
1 pound grated processed cheddar cheese (4 cups)
3/4 cup beer
dash red pepper
1 tablespoon dry mustard
1/4 teaspoon salt
1/2 teaspoon worcestershire sauce
1 unbeaten egg

Melt butter in top of double boiler over boiling water. Slowly stir in cheese. As the cheese melts, stir all but 1 tablespoon of beer into it, a little at a time. Combine the next 4 ingredients with the 1 tablespoon of beer. Add the egg, and stir quickly with spoon until smooth. Add to cheese mixture and mix well. Serve at once over crackers, toast or broiled tomato halves.

Mrs. Johnson M. Fortenbaugh

# SCALLOPED CHEESE AND DEVILED HAM

2 cups bread cubes spread with deviled ham
2 ounces cheddar cheese cut in small pieces
2 tablespoons butter
3 eggs slightly beaten
1 tablespoon minced onion
½ teaspoon salt     speck of pepper
2 cups milk

Spread bread slices with deviled ham.
Cut into cubes and measure 2 cups.
Alternate layers of cubes and cheese in
a greased or oiled casserole. Combine
rest of ingredients and pour over bread
mixture. Place in a pan of warm water,
bake in moderate oven 350° for 35
minutes.

Mrs. Johnson M. Fortenbaugh

# TOMATO RAREBIT

One jar American cheese melted in top
of double boiler, add one can tomato soup,
stir with wooden spoon and pour over hot
buttered toast.

Mrs. E. A. Jimenis

# Swiss Cheese Pie

1 pound grated cheese (hard ends may
     be used)
2 eggs
½ - ¾ cup milk
2 tablespoons butter
Paprika

    Fill unbaked pie crust
with grated cheese, milk and
beaten eggs. Dot with butter
and sprinkle with paprika.
Bake in oven (350°) until
crisp and cheese is melted.
Serve immediately!

        Mrs. Ernest J. Heinmuller

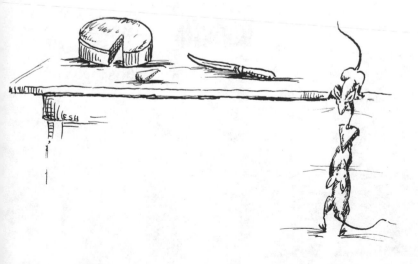

## EGGS BAKED IN BACON RINGS

Fry bacon until partly done but not crisp. Use surplus fat to grease muffin cups. Then place bacon in a circle inside muffin cup. Slip an egg in the center, season with salt and pepper. Bake 15 to 20 minutes in slow moderate oven.

Mrs. Johnson M. Fortenbaugh

## RED BUNNY

3 tablespoons butter
3 tablespoons flour
1 can tomato soup
1/2 tablespoon mustard

1/2 teaspoon salt
3 cups grated cheese
1/4 teaspoon soda

When all the ingredients are melted and blended, add one half pint of cream. When heated add 2 well beaten eggs and 1/4 teaspoon paprika. Serve on ▮▮▮▮ or toast

Edith Adkins

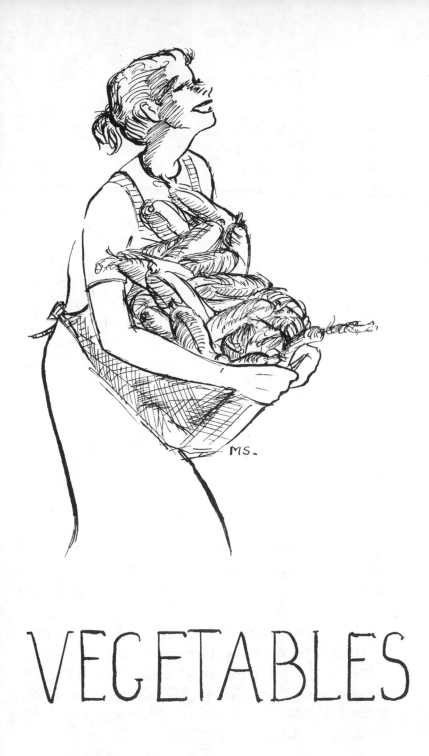

# VEGETABLES

# TOMATO PUDDING

1 10 ounce can tomato puree
1/4 cup boiling water
1/4 teaspoon salt
6 tablespoons brown sugar
1 cup fresh bread crumbs
1/4 cup melted butter

Put tomato puree in a pan, rinse the tin with boiling water and add. Heat to boiling point and add salt and brown sugar.

Place in a greased baking dish, pour butter over bread crumbs and add tomato mixture.

Cover and bake in moderate oven (375°) for half hour.

Mrs. C. E. Partridge

# FRIED TOMATOES

Grate stale bread and season to taste with salt and pepper and a little sugar. Cut firm ripe tomatoes in slices, half inch thick, allowing 3 to 4 slices for each serving. Pat slices in the crumbs on both sides. Have iron spider hot with a generous amount of lard or bacon grease. When grease is bubbling, carefully lay in slices. Cook slowly, turn with spatula when brown. When second side is brown remove at once from frying pan. Serve with bacon strips.

Helen Lloyd

# SCALLOPED TOMATOES

2½ cups canned tomatoes

1 cup dry bread cubes

1 tablespoon minced onion

¼ cup butter

1 tablespoon flour

1 teaspoon pepper

1 tablespoon sugar

1 teaspoon dry mustard

2 slices buttered bread

Combine tomatoes, bread cubes and onions. Melt butter; add flour, seasonings and mustard. Add tomatoe mixture and pour into greased 1½ quart baking dish. Square Pyrex shallow one is good. Cut bread slices in cubes; sprinkle over tomatoes. Bake in hot oven 400° for 30 minutes. Serves 6. If bread is not dry, toast before combining.

Mrs. Thomas T. Firth

# CREAMED FRIED TOMATOES

Slice Tomatoes, put salt, sugar and flour on them. Have frying pan hot, with bacon fat, brown until they fall apart, then stir them altogether and let cook awhile. Add cream and stir. You may use canned tomatoes drained first. This may be used for breakfast or luncheon with toast and bacon.

Mrs. Douglas Hanks

# TOMATOES IN SOUR CREAM

3 good sized tomatoes
2 tablespoons butter
salt, pepper

Sugar
Worcestershire sauce
½ cup sour cream

Cut tomatoes into small pieces and sauté in butter until soft. Salt, pepper and sugar them to taste. Add a dash of Worcestershire sauce. Stir in sour cream and serve on toast.

Mrs. C. C. Koehn

# HARRIET'S BAKED TOMATOES

6 to 8 firm tomatoes, sliced
1 green pepper
3 sliced onions
salt

Place layer of tomatoes, peppers and onions in greased casserole, sprinkle with brown sugar and cracker crumbs. Repeat until casserole is filled, crumbs on top and dot with butter. Cook in hot oven 40 to 45 minutes.

Mae P. Stewart

# SWEET POTATOES WITH APPLES

6 large apples (tart)
5 medium sweet potatoes
½ cup butter
1 cup sugar
1 cup hot water

Boil potatoes, and cut in thick slices. Core apples and slice thickly. Place a layer of potatoes in baking dish, dot with butter, sprinkle with sugar, then add a layer of apples. Continue alternating potatoes, apples, butter and sugar till all are used. Pour cup of hot water over all, and bake in 375° oven half hour or until apples are done.

Mrs. Thomas Hughes

# SWEET POTATO SOUFFLE

2 cups cooked, mashed sweet potatoes
1 cup hot milk                    2 eggs
2 tablespoons sugar     1 tablespoon nutmeg
½ tablespoon salt          ½ cup raisins
2 tablespoon butter       ½ cup chopped walnuts
            few marshmallows

Scald milk. In it dissolve sugar, salt, and butter. Add this mixture to the potatoes and beat until light and fluffy. Add beaten egg yolks; then nutmeg, raisins and nuts. Beat whites stiff and cut and fold them lightly into mixture. Pour into buttered baking dish, placing marshmallows on top. Bake in moderate oven (about ¾ of hour) until the souffle's set and marshmallows browned. Serve at once

Instead of nutmeg and marshmallows, this souffle may be flavored with 2 tablespoons sherry or brandy.
It may be baked in unbaked pie shell and served warm.

                        Mrs. John W. Noble

# SWEET POTATO PUFFS

2 cups mashed sweet potatoes
1 egg (beaten)
1/2 teaspoon salt
1/2 teaspoon pepper
8 marshmallows
1/2 cup crushed cornflakes

Add salt and pepper to potatoes. Add beaten egg. If mixture is dry add a little milk. Form into 8 balls with a marshmallow inside of each. Roll in flakes. Keep fry in hot fat or bake in moderate oven.

Mrs. Frank Teelease

# BUBBLE AND SQUEAK

Melt butter in skillet, add sliced cooked potatoes, chopped cooked cabbage and pepper and salt to taste. Turn with spatula occasionally, till nicely browned. Serve piping hot.

Mrs. Edward T. Bromfield

# GARLIC POTATOES

6 servings of cooked white potatoes
1/4 cup butter
1 clove finely minced garlic
2 teaspoons paprika
salt and pepper
1/4 cup olive oil
small amount cream

Simmer garlic and seasonings for a few minutes in the butter. Add olive oil. Beat this and cream into mashed potatoes.

Mrs. Carroll Elder

=== = === = === = === = === = ===:

# LEFT-OVER POTATOES

Dice boiled potatoes, place in baking dish and cover with white sauce made with cheese. Place buttered crumbs on top and brown in a moderate oven.

Mrs. Wyatt D. Pickering

# PREPARATION of MACARONI

The macaroni put in a pan
Cover with water as fast as you can
Then boil until with a fork 'twill pierce
Not letting, of course, your fire too fierce
Then take from the pan and cut up small
Season with pepper and salt, that's all
Put back in the pan with savory cheese
The quantity being "as much as you please"
Add butter — surely enough to taste
Cover with milk, don't spill in haste
Boil gently until the cheese you dissolve
Pour into the dish with cast iron resolve.
Grate neatly some bread crumbs o'er the dish
Put into the oven and brown as you wish.

Mrs. Anna M. Fountain

\\\ /// \\\ /// \\\ /// \\\ /// \\\ /// \\\ /// \\\ /// \\\ /// \\\ /// \\\ ///

## FLUFFY BOILED RICE

1 cup rice (white or brown)
1½ cups boiling water

Boil water in top of double boiler, add salt, then rice, and boil directly over flame 10 minutes. Place over boiling water in lower part of double boiler and cook until rice is tender. Cover with a linen towel. Rice may be kept hot and fluffy for a long time this way.

Mrs. George D. Olds, III

# Rice Savory With Herbs

1 cup uncooked rice
2 tablespoons Wesson Oil
2 tablespoons butter
1 small onion minced
1 clove garlic
2 tablespoons white wine
1/2 teaspoon salt
1 teaspoon paprika
1/2 teaspoon parsley
1/2 teaspoon savory
4 bouillon cubes
4 cups water

Rub uncooked rice clean with a dry towel, but do not wash. Mix and heat oil and butter in a skillet or earthenware casserole. Add onion, garlic and rice. Fry over slow fire until rice is brown, stirring frequently. Then add wine, seasonings and green herbs, stir well. Dissolve bouillon cubes in hot water. Pour a cup of it over the rice. Stir once, then cover tightly. Cook slowly until the bouillon is absorbed, then add another cup. Continue this process until rice is tender and bouillon is used up. Don't stir after first bouillon is added. Makes four large servings

Mrs. Orthur Keegan

# ITALIAN RICE

2 tablespoons butter
½ cup raw rice
2 cups chicken stock
¼ cup grated cheese
⅛ teaspoon paprika
⅛ teaspoon pepper

Melt butter, add rice and sauté for 1 minute. Heat the 2 cups of chicken stock to boiling point and pour over the rice. Add cheese, paprika and pepper and bake in casserole in 350° oven for 1 hour. Cover for last 30 minutes if necessary. Serves 4

Mrs. William H. Norris

# GREEN PEPPER AND RICE CASSEROLE

3 or 4 green peppers
1 Cup rice
1 can condensed tomato soup
1 teaspoon Worcestershire sauce
1/4 pound cheese, diced

Cook peppers in a small amount of salted water until partially done. Boil rice, drain. Add diced cheese and cover until cheese melts. Then add can condensed tomato soup with Worcestershire sauce.

Drain peppers, place in casserole and cover with rice mixture. Bake in moderate oven 350° for 45 minutes.

Mrs. Douglas Hanks

# ITALIAN SPAGHETTI

1 pound round steak, ground
1/2 pound suet - whole
1 large can tomatoes
3 green peppers
3 or 4 cloves garlic
3 pimientoes
1/2 pound mushrooms
2 cups parsley
1/2 pound butter
1 cup white wine
1/2 cup sherry
1 cup brandy (optional)

Keep suet whole and remove when sauce is done. Put meat, peppers, garlic, mushrooms, pimientoes and parsley through the meat grinder. Brown meat slightly in butter in heavy skillet. Add remaining ingredients and simmer slowly for 2 hours. The brandy improves the flavor, but is expensive. It is very good with just sherry. Serve with cooked thin spaghetti and plenty q Parmesan cheese.

Oliver Grymes

# BAKED MACARONI LOAF

1½ cups elbow macaroni
3 quarts boiling water
4 teaspoons salt

Boil 9 minutes, drain and rinse with boiling water.

3 cups milk
⅓ cup butter or margarine
2 cups soft bread crumbs
⅓ cup chopped pimientoes
3 cups grated American cheese
⅓ cup minced parsley
¼ cup minced onion
Salt and pepper to taste
6 beaten eggs

Scald milk and butter together, add all ingredients except eggs. Mix well, then add macaroni and eggs, stirring until well blended. Pour into loaf pan, bake in 325° oven for 1 hour 10 minutes. Cool 10 minutes and unmold. Serve with mushroom sauce.

Serves 8.

Mrs. C.E. Partridge

# MACARONI, ITALIAN STYLE

| | |
|---|---|
| 1¼ cups butter | 1 large onion, chopped fine |
| ½ tablespoon bread crumbs | 1 teaspoon salt |
| ¾ pound macaroni, cooked | ¼ teaspoon pepper |
| 1⅓ cups thick tomato pulp | 3 eggs, beaten |
| 1½ cups tomato juice | 1½ cups rich milk and cream |
| ¾ pound smoked ham, cubed | 2 tablespoons Parmesan |
| 1¼ cups grated Parmesan cheese | cheese, grated |
| 1½ cups fresh mushrooms, diced | 2 Tablespoons butter |
| | 2 Tablespoons bread crumbs |

Butter a casserole well, sprinkle bread crumbs on
top of butter. Put in one layer of macaroni then
a layer of tomato pulp and juice, butter,
cheese, ham, some of the mushrooms and
onions, salt and pepper. Then another layer
of macaroni, so forth, until the form is
¾ full. Pour eggs with milk and cream over
the whole, loosening macaroni with fork to
allow liquid to mix well with contents. Top
with cheese, butter and bread crumbs. Bake
in moderate oven (350° - 375°) for thirty-
forty minutes. Serves four.

Mrs. Francis G. Bartlett

"Red pepper in your shoes prevents
chills."

# HOMINY AU GRATIN

Empty a can of drained hominy into a frying pan and pour in some milk to loosen the kernels. Keep stirring even though it seems discouraging for 5 minutes or so. Then make a rich cream sauce (½ pint cream is helpful) season well and stir in ¼ pound grated sharp cheese. Mix hominy and sauce — it should be runny; it's not good if dry.

When thoroughly mixed, put it in a deep pyrex dish or casserole, cover with grated cheese and plenty of paprika. Put in hot oven until it sizzles. Run under the broiler if you like the top crispy.

This with bacon and fried tomatoes makes a satisfying meal.

Jack Gill

# Corn Pudding

12 ears golden bantam corn
2 eggs separated
butter, size of an egg
1 cup cream
Salt and pepper

Score and scrape the cooked corn. Salt and pepper to taste. Beat egg whites till stiff, beat egg yolks till lemon colored. Place ingredients in greased baking dish, folding in whites last, and bake ½ hour, in oven, 375°. Serves 6 - 8.

Mrs. Charles Todd

---

## Acorn Squash Baked

Halve squash and fill cavity with brown sugar, spreading over cut side to shell. Dot with butter, season and bake in moderate oven until tender (45 minutes).

Clem Snsath

# CORN FRITTERS

1 cup grated corn     Salt
3 eggs (separated)     Pepper
1 teaspoon flour

Mix corn, egg yolks, flour, salt and pepper. Beat egg whites and fold into mixture. Drop by tablespoon into hot frying pan. Fry in medium amount of lard.

Mrs. Ernest J. Heinmuller

# SQUASH FRITTERS

2 medium size squash     ¼ teaspoon salt
1 egg     ¼ teaspoon baking
1 tablespoonful of sugar     powder
1 cup flour     dash of pepper
¼ cup milk

Beat egg, grate squash. Add flour, salt, baking powder, milk, sugar, and pepper. Mix well. Drop by spoonfuls into hot frying pan. Yields about 10 or 12 fritters. If more is desired, double quanity.

Mrs. Russell Hallowell

# Summer Squash with Green Peppers

2 medium sized Summer Squash
⅓ cup olive oil
6 medium sized green peppers (seeded)
1 cup tomato pulp
½ teaspoon salt
⅛ teaspoon pepper

Wash, scrape and dry squash. Remove seeds and cut in 3 inch strips. Heat olive oil in pan and fry squash until brown. Then remove from oil and brown peppers on all sides. While in pan, cut them in strips and remove draining off the oil.

Allow 3 tablespoons of oil to remain in pan, pour in tomato pulp, cover and simmer for 15 minutes.

Add squash, peppers and seasoning. Cook 3 minutes longer over low flame. Serves 4.

Mrs. Francis G. Bartlett

# CARROT SOUFFLÉ

1 bunch carrots (4 to 6)
1 tablespoon butter
1 or 2 eggs
1 heaping tablespoon flour

Cook carrots in salt water. Save 1 cup of the carrot water. Mash carrots through sieve.
Put flour and carrot water in double boiler, add butter just before it thickens. Remove from stove, immediately add egg yolks well beaten.
Let cool and mix with carrots. Fold in egg whites beaten very light. Put in casserole and bake 25 minutes in 350° oven

Nellie R. Wrightson

# CARROT LOAF

12 carrots
1 slice of bread broken into small pieces
1 or 2 eggs
1 tablespoon grated onion          salt
1 tablespoon sugar                 pepper
2 tablespoons butter or bacon drippings

Cook carrots, drain, mash and stir in rest of ingredients. Pack in greased casserole, sprinkle with parsley, and bake in moderate oven until nicely browned, 30 minutes or more.

Virginia C. Couer

## Carrots with Herbs

Wash two bunches of young carrots, split in two lengthwise. Put them in saucepan with 2 tablespoons of butter, 2 lettuce leaves, 2 tablespoons of boiling water and 1 teaspoon of sugar. Sauté them by shaking the pan and stirring them occassionally. Add $\frac{1}{4}$ teaspoon of salt, a dash of pepper, chopped parsley and $\frac{1}{4}$ teaspoon of tarragon. Add 2 tablespoons of cream and serve.

Mrs. Arthur Keegan

# STRING BEANS and ALMONDS

1 quart string beans
4 tablespoons butter
1/4 pound blanched almonds

Cook string beans for 20 minutes in boiling salted water. Sauté the almonds in the melted butter, and add to the drained beans.

Let stand for 1/2 hour so that the flavor of the nuts permeates the beans.

Serves 4.

Mrs. Frank Gunther

# BOILED CUCUMBERS

Quarter cucumbers lengthwise and cook in salted water until done (about 15 minutes).

Make a cream sauce or use sour cream to cover.

Dot with parsley and serve.

Mr. Conway Hodges

SALADS

and

ms.

DRESSINGS

# TOMATO ASPIC

Bring to a boil 1 number 2 can of tomatoes. Dissolve in it 1 package of lemon gelatine. Add:

  1 teaspoon onion juice
  ¼ teaspoon ground cloves
  ½ cup chopped celery
  ½ cup chopped pecans

Pour into molds and chill.

Virginia C. Cover

∧∨∧∨∧∨∧∨∧∨∧∨∧∨∧∨∧∨∧∨∧∨∧

# SIMPLE TOMATO ASPIC

3 envelopes plain gelatine
2 cans V-8 juice

Soak gelatine in ¼ or more cups of juice. Heat the remaining juice to boiling point, dissolve gelatine in it. Cool, pour into mold and chill. Serve with mayonnaise mixed with French dressing.

Mrs. John G. Shannahan, Jr.

# JELLIED TOMATO SALAD

1 can tomatoes (# 2½)
½ bay leaf
3 cloves
½ chopped onion
1 teaspoon salt
1 stalk celery
few grains cayenne
1 tablespoon vinegar or lemon juice
1½ teaspoon sugar (if desired)
1½ tablespoon gelatine
dash Worcestershire

Soak gelatine in ¼ cup cold water for 10 minutes. Mix tomatoes, salt, celery, onion, pepper, bay leaf, and cloves. Simmer for 20 minutes. Strain and add vinegar or lemon juice, sugar, and Worcestershire. Add gelatine, stir until dissolved and pour into mold which has been rinsed in cold water. Chill and unmold onto salad greens and serve with mayonnaise or french dressing. Serves 6.

Mrs. Harvey Jarboe

## Potage De Salade

Peel 8 fully ripe red or yellow tomatoes. Cut into thin half-moon sections. Mix with the following:

½ cup diced celery
¼ cup minced onion
½ cup diced green pepper
Pinch salt, pepper, parsley
Pinch of tabasco
pinch of cayenne
½ teaspoon curry
½ cup mayonaise
3 tablespoons French dressing
3 tablespoons sour cream

Serve ice-cold as a first course in a lettuce cup. Serves 6.

Mrs. Arthur Keegan

To the best cook goes the whole tomato.

# MOLDED SALAD

Serves 25

4 cups condensed tomato soup
8 tablespoons lemon juice
4 packages lemon gelatine
2 cups boiling water
4 tablespoons finely cut onion
2 teaspoons salt
4 packages cream cheese
2 cups sliced stuffed olives
2 cups mayonnaise
2 cups cream

Dissolve gelatine in boiling water, add tomato soup, and other ingredients, softening the cream cheese with the cream.

Mrs. Robert C. Morris

# STRINGBEAN SALAD

1 can stringbeans

French Dressing:
   2 parts oil
   1 part vinegar
   salt
   pepper
   paprika
   dash lemon juice
   onion, chopped very fine

Heat stringbeans and while still hot, pour French Dressing over. Be sure you have an ample amount of onion. Chill in refrigerator until ready for serving. Serve on lettuce.

Mrs. Ernest J. Heinmuller

# Avacado, Ripe (Huacamole)

Remove seed. Scoop out meat carefully, leaving skin intact.

Mix meat with following:

1½ Teaspoons Lea & Perrins sauce.

2 tablespoons mayonnaise.

1 teaspoon chopped onion.

1 Teaspoon chili sauce.

Dash cayenne pepper.

Replace mixture into skin; garnish and serve.

A small portion of Roquefort cheese can be added if you like it.

Mr. Frank Gregson —

## Bishop's Salad

Break up enough lettuce and endive for 4. Chop finely the yolk of 4 hardboiled eggs. Add 12 tablespoons of finely chopped Blue cheese, add to egg yolks and combine with lettuce.

Cut an onion in half and rub the surface over 4 pieces of buttered melba toast, then cut into small pieces and add to the lettuce. Toss with the following dressing:

Into a large 10 ounce container put 1/3 cup of mayonaise, 1/3 cup sour cream (or sweet cream and 1/3 cup Herb vinegar. Add one rounded tablespoon of sugar, and salt and pepper to taste.

Mrs. Arthur Keegar

# JELLIED HAM LOAF

1½ tablespoons unflavored gelatine
¼ cup cold water
1 10½ ounce can condensed tomato soup
1 cup water
1 package cream cheese (3 ounce)
½ cup mayonnaise or salad dressing
2 teaspoons prepared mustard
2 tablespoons lemon juice
2 cups cooked ground ham

Soften gelatine in ¼ cup water. Heat tomato soup and water, add gelatine and softened cream cheese; stir until dissolved. Cool until almost set; add remaining ingredients; mix. Chill until firm in mold garnished with stuffed olive slices. Serves 8 – 10

Can be made day before using.

Mrs. Kenneth B. Millett

# HAM MOUSSE

2 cups chopped ham
2 teaspoons sweet pickle
1 cup mayonnaise
2 tablespoons gelatine
1 cup cold water
2 hard boiled eggs

Soften gelatine in 1/4 cup cold water, heat the remaining water and dissolve gelatine in it. When cool, put 1/4 cup gelatine in mold and line bottom and sides with sliced eggs. Add rest of gelatine to ham, pickle, and mayonnaise and pour in mold after first gelatine is firm.

Ethel Chapman Judd

## Golden Glow Salad

| | |
|---|---|
| 1 cup boiling water | 1/3 cup nuts |
| 1 cup pineapple juice | 1 tablespoon vinegar |
| 1 package lemon jello | 1/2 teaspoon salt |
| 1 cup diced pineapple | 1 cup grated carrots |

Canned pineapple and juice must be used. Dissolve jello in boiling water. Add juice and salt. When slightly thickened, add pineapple, carrots and nuts. Turn into mold until firm.

Mrs. Marcus Borden-Smith

# JELLIED CRANBERRY SALAD

1 package lemon gelatine
1 cup boiling water
2 teaspoons lemon juice
1 cup (½ can) cranberry sauce
½ cup drained crushed pineapple
1 cup diced celery

Dissolve gelatine in water, add the lemon juice. Chill, and when slightly thickened, fold in remaining ingredients. Turn into molds and chill until firm. Unmold on lettuce and serve salad dressing or mayonnaise with it.

Mrs. Leland Shook

=================

## JELLIED FRUIT SLICE

Cut as many grapefruit in half as desired. Cut sections of fruit out and drain. Remove pulp and membrane from shells. Fill clean shells with any flavor jello desired. Place in refrigerator until almost firm. Add grapefruit sections and a few maraschino cherries, cut. Chill until very firm. Slice thinly for salad, or serve ¼ grapefruit as first course or topped with whipped cream as dessert.

Mrs. Thomas M. Carpenter

# MIXED HERB VINEGAR

Loosely fill quart jar with mint leaves, basil, tarragon, burnet and chives. Fill jar with wine or cider vinegar and cover tightly. Use wax paper to line metal cover. Shake well and keep in cool (not cold) place for 10 days.

Mrs. E.A. Jimenis

---

# FRENCH DRESSING

½ cup sugar  
1½ teaspoons salt  
1 cup olive oil  
1½ teaspoons paprika  
1 teaspoon dry mustard  
1½ cups vinegar  
  (use tarragon, herb or garlic vinegar)  
Blend dry ingredients, add vinegar and oil. Beat 5 minutes.

Mrs. Robert G. Henry

---

# COLE SLAW DRESSING

2 eggs  
1 cup milk  
Pinch paprika  
1 cup hot vinegar  
5 tablespoons sugar  
1 teaspoon salt  
1 teaspoon mustard sauce  
3 tablespoons flour  

Mix dry ingredients, eggs and milk. Cook in double boiler until thick, add vinegar. Pour over cabbage - cool

Anne B. Perry

# SURPRISE SAUCE

6 tablespoons mayonnaise
4 tablespoons chili sauce
3 tablespoons tarragon vinegar
1 tablespoon garlic vinegar
1 teaspoon dry mustard
1 teaspoon salt
freshly ground pepper
2 teaspoons capers (optional)

Mix together thoroughly and serve with crab, shrimp, or lobster salad.

James R. Speer, Jr.

# FRENCH DRESSING

1 can condensed tomato soup
3/4 cup vinegar          dash cayenne
3/4 cup salad oil        1/2 tsp. paprika
1 tablespoon Worcestershire
1 tablespoon dry mustard
1/2 cup sugar
1 tablespoon chopped onion
1/2 clove garlic, finely chopped
2 1/2 teaspoons salt

Mix thoroughly - and shake before using.

Mrs. H. Stuart Hammond

# Chicken Salad Dressing

1 quart milk
1½ cups chicken fat
5 egg yolks
2 egg whites
1¼ cup vinegar
2 Teaspoons mustard
½ Teaspoon red pepper
1 tablespoon salt
6 tablespoons flour

Scald the milk. Add the chicken fat, stirring hard. Beat The egg yolks and the whites and add to the milk. Mix the dry ingredients, add vinegar, Then add gradually To the hot mixture. This recipe makes ½ gallon.

Mrs. James Willis —

Sauces

# STEAK SAUCE

2 round tablespoons butter or margarine
1 slightly round teaspoon chopped fresh ginger root
1 medium or 2 small onions
1 tablespoon soya sauce
2 tablespoons Worcestershire sauce

Cook butter, onion and ginger until onions brown a bit, then add soya sauce and Worcestershire sauce and simmer 5 minutes or longer. (optional, add garlic clove and remove before serving).

Put 1/2 of sauce on one side of steak and broil. Add other half to other side and broil. Do not add salt until served.

Willard S. Rousse

# EPICUREAN SAUCE

3 tablespoons mayonaaise
2 tablespoons horseradish
1/2 to 1 teaspoon mustard
1/2 cup heavy cream
1/2 tablespoon salt
few grains cayenne

Beat the cream until stiff and then fold in the other ingredients.

Mrs. S. N. Hersloff

# HARD SAUCE

1 pound XXXX sugar
1/4 pound butter (not margarine)
4 ounces Rum or Whisky

Cream sugar and butter. Add liquor
slowly, beating hard all the time.
Keep in a cool place until ready to
serve on hot Plum Pudding.

Mrs. T. C. Kirby

# BUTTERSCOTCH SAUCE

1 cup brown sugar
1 cup heavy cream
1 teaspoon butter
1 teaspoon vanilla
pinch of salt

Cook until of thick syrup consistency, all
ingredients except vanilla (20 minutes or
more). Add vanilla. Keep warm over hot
water.

Mrs. Elijah Nostrand

250

# CHOCOLATE SAUCE

1 cup sugar
½ cup water
¼ cup butter
1 tablespoon flour
2 squares chocolate
1 teaspoon vanilla
pinch of salt

Dissolve chocolate, butter, and flour over low flame. Add sugar and water and stir. Boil 15 minutes. Remove from fire, add salt and vanilla.

Mrs. Thurston Harrison

# LEMON SAUCE

2 cups sugar
Butter, size of egg
6 tablespoons lemon juice
grated rind of 2 lemons
2 eggs
1 cup boiling water

Place all ingredients except water in double boiler. Add the water very slowly, stirring constantly until well mixed. Cook in double boiler until it thickens, stirring occasionally. Perfect for puddings.

Mrs. W. Mitchell Price

# HARTFORD PUDDING

| | |
|---|---|
| 1 cup bread crumbs | 1 cup currants |
| 1 cup flour | 1 teaspoon baking powder |
| 1 cup sugar | ¼ teaspoon salt |
| 1 cup milk | ½ nutmeg |
| 1 cup chopped suet | 1 teaspoon ginger |
| 1 cup seeded raisins | 1 teaspoon cinnamon |

Mix flour, baking powder, bread crumbs, sugar and milk. Add fruits, suet and spices. Put in can or bag and immerse in boiling water. Boil 4 hours. Serve with hard sauce.

Mrs. James H. Willis

# DATE PUDDING

| | |
|---|---|
| 3 eggs | 1 cup chopped English walnuts |
| ¾ cup sugar | ½ teaspoon baking powder |
| ½ pound chopped dates | 2 tablespoons flour |

Mix altogether in order given, sifting flour and baking powder, adding pinch salt. Bake in shallow buttered tin. When cold, just before serving cut into squares large enough for individual service. Pour sherry over it to flavor, but not soggy. Fill top evenly with whipped cream and serve.

Mrs. Claire Lappen

# CHERRY PUDDING

2 tablespoons butter or margarine
1¼ cups sugar
1 cup sifted all-purpose flour
1 teaspoon baking powder
⅛ teaspoon salt
¾ cup milk
1½ cups cooked or canned cherries
¼ cup cherry juice

Cream together butter or margarine and 1 cup sugar. Sift together flour, baking powder and salt; add alternately with milk to creamed mixture. Pour into greased baking dish. Combine cherries with remaining sugar and juice, and heat. Pour mixture over batter. Bake in moderate oven 350° 35 to 40 minutes. Serve warm from dish. Serves 6-8.

Mrs. P. N. Horne

# Apricot Snow

2 cups unsweetened stewed apricot pulp
3 egg whites
½ cup granulated sugar
2 tablespoons lemon juice
¼ teaspoon cinnamon

Press fruit through sieve or food mill.
Beat egg whites until stiff. Add sugar,
lemon juice and cinnamon to pulp, mixing
thoroughly. Fold in beaten egg whites.
Serve with chilled Custard Sauce, using
3 leftover egg yolks.

## Custard Sauce

Pinch salt
4 tablespoons granulated sugar
4 teaspoons flour
3 egg yolks beaten
2 cups bottled milk
1 teaspoon vanilla

Mix salt, sugar and flour in top of double
boiler; add egg and blend; then add the
milk and cook over boiling water, stirring
until thickened, about 5 minutes. Cool.
Add vanilla. Makes 2 cups.

Mrs. J. B. Powell

# BROWNIE PUDDING

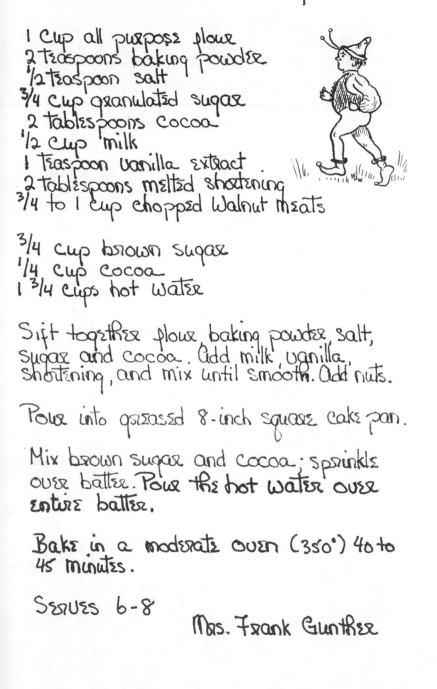

1 cup all purpose flour
2 teaspoons baking powder
1/2 teaspoon salt
3/4 cup granulated sugar
2 tablespoons cocoa
1/2 cup milk
1 teaspoon vanilla extract
2 tablespoons melted shortening
3/4 to 1 cup chopped walnut meats

3/4 cup brown sugar
1/4 cup cocoa
1 3/4 cups hot water

Sift together flour, baking powder, salt,
sugar and cocoa. Add milk, vanilla,
shortening, and mix until smooth. Add nuts.

Pour into greased 8-inch square cake pan.

Mix brown sugar and cocoa; sprinkle
over batter. Pour the hot water over
entire batter.

Bake in a moderate oven (350°) 40 to
45 minutes.

Serves 6-8

Mrs. Frank Gunther

# ORANGE SOUFFLÉ

3 egg whites
3 tablespoons granulated sugar
2 tablespoons orange marmalade
1/4 teaspoon orange extract
1/2 cup chopped toasted almonds

Beat egg whites to a stiff foam. Gradually add sugar, and continue beating until mixture forms peaks.

Add orange marmalade and extract. Pour into the greased top of a double boiler. Place over hot water, cover, and cook 1 hour.

Turn out on a warm serving plate and pour foamy sauce over it.

## FOAMY SAUCE

3 egg yolks
3/4 cup confectioners sugar
1/2 teaspoon vanilla
1/8 teaspoon salt
1 cup heavy cream whipped

Beat the egg yolks, and add the next three ingredients. Fold in the heavy cream. Chill. Sprinkle with nut meats.

Serves 4 to 6

Mrs. Frank Gunther

# NOVA SCOTIA
# STEAMED STRAWBERRY PUDDING

½ cup butter, creamed
1 tablespoon sugar
2 eggs, well beaten
1½ cups flour
1 teaspoon soda
1 cup strawberry preserves

Cream butter, add sugar gradually. Add well-beaten eggs. Mix and sift flour, soda, and pinch of salt and add. Add preserves. Steam over double boiler, for 1½ hours.

### Sauce
¼ cup butter
1 cup sugar
1 beaten egg
½ cup strawberry preserves

Mrs. R. S. Jones

# FIG PUDDING

½ pound figs
1 cup bread crumbs
½ pound sugar
1 cup butter or margarine
5 ounces candied orange peel and citron
1 teaspoon grated nutmeg
5 eggs - well beaten

Combine the sugar and the butter; add the figs and citron, then the bread crumbs. Beat the eggs very well, and fold into the dry mixture.
Steam for 4 hours.

Mrs. S. N. Hersloff

# PRUNE SOUFFLÉ

18 large prunes
1 cup confectioners sugar
8 egg whites, beaten stiff
1 teaspoon vanilla

Steam the prunes until soft.
Pit and chop very fine. Mix in
the sugar and fold in the beaten
egg whites and vanilla.

Pour into buttered casserole
and bake in 250° oven for 30
minutes.

Serve cold with whipped cream.

Betty Jean Wheeler

# Peach Cobbler

Enough peaches to line baking dish
1¼ cups white sugar
⅓ cup butter
½ cup flour

Rub all ingredients together and
place over halved peaches in
baking dish. Cook until mixture
is golden brown and crisp.
Temperature 350°
If using apples, one level Tablespoon
of cinnamon and ¼ cup water.

Mrs. Robert C. Morris —

# LEMON PUDDING

1 Tablespoon butter
1 cup sugar
2 Tablespoons flour
1½ lemons - juice and grated rind
1 cup milk
3 egg yolks

Cream butter and sugar together, add flour, juice and rind of lemons, milk and yolks of eggs. Beat whites of eggs until stiff and fold into mixture. Bake in a pan of hot water for one hour, very slowly. (about 250°)

Mrs. Joseph T. White

# CHRISTMAS PUDDING

1 pound carrots          1 pound flour
¾ pound suet             1 cup milk
1 pound raisins          1 teaspoon baking powder
½ pound currants         pinch of salt

Mix all ingredients after first having
cooked and mashed the carrots. Do not
make mixture too soft, add bit more flour.
Put into greased coffee can with top.
Cook in boiling water for 3 hrs. Cool and
then cook 3 hours longer.

## SAUCE FOR PUDDING

¼ pound butter      2 teaspoons hot water
2 cups brown sugar     2 egg yolks

Cream butter and sugar. Add boiling hot
water. Add 2 egg yolks well beaten. Put
in top of double boiler and cook for 25
minutes. Add grated rind and juice of 1
lemon. Beat.
Add jigger of brandy as you serve.

Mrs. John G. Rouse

# CHOCOLATE PUDDING

2 cups bread crumbs
2 cups milk
4 squares chocolate
5 egg yolks
1 cup sugar
2 teaspoonfuls baking powder

Meringue:
5 egg whites
1 cup sugar

Soak the crumbs in the milk. Pour this into melted chocolate mixed with the eggs, sugar, and baking powder. Put in baking pan and dot the top with butter. Bake until a silver knife comes out clean. While hot spread the top with jelly and then meringue. Place in oven again and brown.

Mrs. Ida M. Leonard

# BAKED BANANAS IN RUM

6 bananas (West Indies cooking type preferred)
4 tablespoons butter or lard
¼ cup water     1 stick cinnamon
1 cup rum     1 cup water

Brown bananas in shortening; pour off surplus. Put bananas in pyrex dish; add water, rum, sugar and stick cinnamon. Place in 400° oven, bake till liquid becomes syrupy. Serve.

━━ ━━ ━━ ━━ ━━ ━━ ━━ ━━ ━━

# PAJANOS TEMPACION (BANANAS TEMPTATION)

6 bananas (West Indies cooking type preferred)
4 tablespoons butter or lard
1 cup red wine     ½ cup water
1 cup sugar     1 stick cinnamon

Brown bananas in shortening until golden brown, drain off excess fat. Add wine, sugar, water and cinnamon. Let simmer until liquid becomes syrupy.

These are delicious served with Arroz-Con Pollo.

Mrs. Alfred Lacazette

# Bananas with Coconut

6 medium sized bananas, quartered
      lengthwise and cut across
      in 2 inch pieces.
1½ tablespoons butter
½ cup honey
⅛ teaspoon salt
1½ teaspoon lemon juice
1 cup grated coconut
24 soft lady fingers
⅓ cup whipping cream

Peel and prepare ripe, firm
bananas. Put in pan with butter and
fry until golden brown. Grease baking
dish, put in honey and melt. Lay
bananas in honey and add salt and
lemon juice. Mix.

Allow to cook over low fire.
Fold ¾ the freshly grated coconut
into banana mixture and spread
thickly on 12 lady fingers. Lay
remaining lady fingers on top, sprinkle
remaining coconut over sides of
spread. Cover and allow to ripen
and chill at least 6 hours.

When ready to serve,
garnish over top with whipped cream.
Serves 6

Mrs. Francis G. Bartlett

# Cream Puffs

½ cup butter or margerine    1 cup flour
1 cup boiling water      4 eggs

Add butter to water and heat over a low flame until butter melts. Add all the flour at once. Stir vigorously until ball forms in the center of the pan. Cool slightly.

Add eggs one at a time, beating after each addition. Mixture should be very stiff.

Shape on a buttered cookie sheet. You may drop the mixture from a spoon.

Bake in hot oven 400° for 35 to 40 minutes. Yields 10 puffs.

## Filling

2 cups milk      ⅔ cup sugar
½ cup flour      2 eggs
½ teaspoon salt      2 tablespoon rum or
       1 tablespoon vanilla

Scald milk. Mix the flour, sugar, salt, and eggs. Add the scalded milk, and cook in the top of a double boiler until the mixture thickens, stirring constantly. Add flavoring and cool.

Mrs. D.C. Kirby

# CHARLOTTE RUSSE

Dissolve 1 ounce gelatine in 1 pint of milk by boiling. Beat yolks of 3 eggs, sweeten to taste and stir into milk on stove. When cooked to a custard, strain into bowl and flavor with vanilla.

Whip 1 quart of double cream and flavor with sherry wine. Whip to a stiff froth. Add this to custard just as it begins to congeal. Add pecan nuts, chopped. Set in a pan to stiffen.

This is especially pretty if a bit of green coloring is added.

Mrs. R. Ellis Clark

## LEMON BISQUE

1 large can evaporated milk
1 package lemon jello
1¼ cup boiling water
¾ cup sugar        pinch of salt
5 tablespoons lemon juice
grated rind of 1 lemon


2 cups vanilla wafer or graham cracker crumbs

Chill milk in freezing unit until it begins
to freeze. Dissolve jello in hot water and
cool in refrigerator. When milk has begun to
freeze, put in mixing bowl and whip until
thick. Add sugar and lemon gradually; fold
in jello.
Put ½ of the crumbs in bottom of 2 nine-
inch pie pans. Spoon mixture onto crumbs.
Sprinkle remaining crumbs on top of mixture
and put in refrigerator until firm.

This dessert may be prepared in a large
freezing tray and frozen .... it may be
made a day ahead of time and is excellent
summer dessert.

                    Mrs. Walter E. Gunby

# LIME ICE

1 box of Lime Jello
1 cup boiling water
1 cup granulated sugar
1 lemon rind grated and juice
2 cups milk
½ pint whipped cream

Dissolve Jello in boiling water; add sugar, let cool, then add milk and juice and rind of lemon. Mix well and place in freezing unit of icebox. When semi-frozen take out and add whipped cream. Return to icebox and refreeze.

Mrs. Joseph T. White

## FRUIT SHERBET

1 cup orange juice  ⅔ to ¾ cup sugar
juice of 1 lemon    2 cups milk

In freezing tray mix fruit juices and sugar.
Let stand about 15 minutes or until dissolved.
Add milk slowly, stirring constantly. Place
in freezing compartment and freeze rapidly.

Variations : For orange juice substitute:
1 cup crushed pineapple
    1 cup crushed strawberries
    1 cup crushed raspberries
        1 cup crushed peaches.

Mrs. D.C. Kirby, Jr.

## ANGEL PARFAIT

1 cup sugar         ¼ cup water
1 pint cream        2 egg whites
    salt and vanilla to taste

Boil the sugar and the water until a thread
can be formed. Add this mixture slowly to
the 2 stiffly beaten egg whites. Beat this
until thick, cool and add salt and vanilla.
Combine this with the cream, whipped until
stiff. Freeze without stirring.

Mrs. William T. Hammond

## ORANGE SHERBET

3/4 cup orange juice
grated rind of one orange
1½ cups granulated sugar
3 cups cold water

Put the water and sugar on to boil, boil for
20 minutes. Meanwhile squeeze the oranges
and soak the grated rind in the juice. Let
the sugar and water cool, then add the orange
juice and rind. Put into freezing tray of refrigerator; mashing the ice at least once during freeze.

Mrs. Howard Bloomfield

## FRUIT ICE CREAM

Melt 20 marshmallows in double boiler for
½ hour. Add juice of 1 lemon. Cool slightly.
Add 1 cup finely chopped fruit. Fold in 1 cup
whipped cream.
Freeze in refrigerator.

Mrs. Willard G. Rouse

# ORANGE MARMALADE WHIP

5 eggs
⅛ Teaspoon salt
5 tablespoons sugar

3 tablespoons Orange
    Marmalade
½ teaspoon Orange extract

Beat whites of eggs add salt until stiff. Fold in gradually sugar, next fold in marmalade and orange extract, bake in a greased pyrex baking dish. Set in a shallow pan of water, bake at 275° for 15 minutes, increase to 300° and bake 30 minutes longer.
Turn out on deep platter and coat sides and top with 1 cup pecan meats chopped very fine, surrounded with sauce.

## Sauce

3 egg yolks
1½ cups heavy cream
⅛ tsp salt

1 cup sugar
1 large tablespoon
    vanilla

Beat egg yolks, salt and sugar until light. Have cream luke warm, add slowly to egg yolk. Cook in double boiler beating with rotary egg beater until thick and smooth, add vanilla.

mrs. John N. Todd

## STRAWBERRY ICE CREAM

1 quart strawberries     2 cups heavy cream
1 cup sugar, granulated     ½ cup cream
2 tablespoons confectioners sugar    pinch of salt
1 teaspoon vanilla

Wash, stem and crush berries with sugar. Heat
to boiling point. Remove from fire, add salt
and cool. Run through purée. Whip cream,
add vanilla and confectioners sugar. Fold the
whipped cream mixture into fruit mixture, pour
into freezing tray and freeze rapidly.

Mrs. Marcus Borden-Smith.

## LEMON SNOW

1 lemon (juice and rind)
1 cup hot water     2 tablespoons cornstarch
1 cup sugar     4 tablespoons cold water
whites of 2 eggs

Combine sugar and cornstarch, mix to paste
with cold water. Add hot water and cook
until thick and glossy. Add lemon juice and rind.
When slightly cool fold into 2 stiffly beaten
egg whites. Chill and serve with custard sauce
made with egg yolks.

Mrs. Louis F. Coffin

# IVORY CREAM

2 cups milk
pinch salt
1 rounded tablespoon gelatine (slightly
   more than 1 envelope)
¼ cup cold water, dissolve gelatine in it
⅓ - ½ cup sugar
1 teaspoon vanilla
1 cup heavy cream

Heat milk, add salt, gelatine, sugar
and vanilla. Cool, set in refrigerator.
When it begins to jell, fold in whipped
cream. Mix until smooth, put into
moulds that have been rinsed in
cold water. Chill. (Good made day
before using.) Serve with crushed
strawberries, fresh or frozen, or
with chocolate or butterscotch sauce
and rolled (crushed) nuts.

Variation: Substitute ½ cup strong
coffee for ½ cup of the 2 cups of
milk. Serve topped with whipped
cream. Garnish with a cherry.

                          Mrs. Elijah Nostrand

# PIE CRUST

1½ cups flour          ½ cup shortening
½ teaspoon salt      4-5 tablespoons cold water

Sift flour and salt together. Cut in shortening
in pieces about size of pea. Add water, tablespoon
at a time, mixing and pressing ingredients
together with a fork until dough is just moist
enough to hold together. Form in two balls
and roll. For 8-9 inch pie.

Mrs. Claire Lappen

# PIE CRUST - NEVER FAIL

1 cup flour          ¼ pound butter
pinch salt          1 cake cream cheese

Work butter and cheese into flour with
your hands. Roll thin with rolling pin.
Line pie plates. Fill with any mixture.

Mrs. W. Mitchell Price

# MERINGUE PIE SHELL

½ cup granulated sugar
⅛ teaspoon cream of tartar
2 egg whites

Sift together sugar and cream of tartar. Beat egg whites until stiff, but moist. Add sugar gradually. Beat until stiff and sugar is dissolved. Grease pie plate well with margerine and line with the meringue. Bake in 275° oven 1 hour. Fill with ice cream or chocolate pudding or crushed fruit, just before serving. Can be made day before needed.

Mae P. Stewart

# RICH PASTRY FOR PIES, TARTS OR CHEESE STRAWS

1 cup flour
1 Teaspoon salt
½ cup shortening
1 Teaspoon sugar
1 teaspoon baking powder
1 egg yolk beaten with
1 tablespoon cold water

Mix dough. Put in ice box to chill. Then roll out.

Cecil D. Cox

# PERSIAN LIME ANGEL PIE

4 egg whites
1/4 teaspoon cream of tartar
1 cup sugar
1/4 teaspoon vanilla

Beat whites and cream of tartar together until they hold up in a peak. Add sugar and vanilla gradually and beat until glossy. Spread on a nine inch pie plate. Bake at 275° for twenty minutes and 300° for forty minutes. Cool before filling.

Lime filling:
4 egg yolks
1/2 cup sugar
5 tablespoons lime juice
2 tablespoons grated lime rind

Beat yolks until thick. Gradually add sugar, juice and rind. Cook in double boiler until thick. Cool and spread over meringue crust. Cover pie with thick whipped cream and cool in refrigerator until time to serve.

Mrs. Robert G. Henry, Jr.

# ANGEL PIE

4 egg whites    ½ teaspoon cream of tartar
1 cup sugar

Beat egg whites until foamy. Then beat
in cream of tartar. Add sugar gradually.
When stiff enough to hold shape spread in
a buttered 9 inch pie plate. Bake at
least 35 minutes at 300°. Cool while
making filling as follows:

4 egg yolks    1 teaspoon grated lemon
¾ cup sugar         rind
3 Tablespoons lemon juice 1 cup whipping cream

Beat egg yolks until thick and lemon colored.
Add sugar, lemon juice and rind. Cook in
double boiler until thick. Cool, then fold in
whipped cream. Pour in meringue shell.
Cool 24 hours in refrigerator before
serving.

Mrs. C. E. Partridge

# LOUISE'S APPLE PIE

½ recipe plain pastry
6-8 tart apples
½ cup brown sugar
1 tablespoon flour
1 tablespoon butter
1 ¼ teaspoons cinnamon
½ cup white sugar
2 tablespoons cream

Line 9 inch pie pan with pastry.
Put pared sliced apples in bowl
and mix with sugars, cinnamon
and flour. Fill crust with apples,
dot with butter, and pour cream
over all.

Do not use top crust, but invert
a pie pan over pie and cook in a
350° oven for 15 minutes. Remove
top and cook 15 minutes more, or
until apples are tender.

Mrs. Charles E. Wheeler

# CANDY APPLE PIE

2 large tart apples
1 cup firmly packed brown sugar
1 cup sifted flour
½ cup butter
¾ ground nuts
1 cup heavy cream

Pare apples and slice thin. Arrange layers in a greased baking dish, sprinkle with ⅓ cup brown sugar, add another layer of apples.

Combine remaining sugar, flour and nuts. Stir into butter gradually, butter creamed soft. Roll or pat into the shape of the dish top, place over the filling, pressing edges down. Gash to permit steam to escape.

Bake in a moderate (350°) oven about one hour. Serve warm with whipped cream. Yields 6 portions.

Mrs. Frank Gregson

CANDY

284

# Lemon Meringue Pie

Juice 4 lemons          5 tablespoons corn starch
3 cups milk             2 cups sugar
8 egg yolks             ¼ pound butter

Squeeze lemons after saving grated rind.
Heat milk. Mix egg yolks and sugar
together. Save whites. Add corn starch
to mixed sugar and yolks. Blend
thoroughly and then mix with heated
milk. Cook until thick, stirring constantly.
When thickened add lemon juice, then
butter. Remove from fire and cool.

### For Meringue

To egg whites add 6 tablespoonsful
cold water. ½ teaspoon cream tarter.
Dash salt - (⅛ teaspoonful). A little
lemon juice (½ tablespoonful). Beat,
then add 12 tablespoonsful sugar, one
at a time beating the mixture well
each time sugar is added, then add
pinch salt and lemon juice.

Mrs. Douglas Hanks

# LEMON CAKE PIE

| | |
|---|---|
| 1 heaping cup sugar | 4 egg yolks |
| ½ cup butter | juice of 2 lemons |
| 1 tablespoon flour | rind of 1 lemon |
| ½ cup milk | 4 egg whites |

Melt butter, add flour mixed with sugar. Add beaten yolks, lemon juice and rind, and milk. Mix well. Fold in beaten egg whites and pour into unbaked pie crust. Bake in moderate oven until browned.

This pie when baked has about an inch of cake texture on top of custard texture lemon filling.

Serve very cold. Excellent served with slightly sweetened whipped cream.

Mrs. John W. Noble

# LEMON SPONGE PIE
## or Lemon Cake-Pie

| | |
|---|---|
| 1 cup sugar | grated rind of 1 lemon |
| dash salt | juice of 2 lemons |
| 1 tablespoon flour | 1 tablespoon melted butter |
| 3 eggs, separated | 1 cup hot milk |

Combine sugar, salt and flour. Add egg yolks, beat
until light. Add lemon rind, juice and butter.
Gradually stir in milk. Fold in egg whites, beaten
until stiff. Turn into pastry lined pie pan (unbaked)
Bake in a moderately slow oven (325°) until
pie is firm. Approximate yield: 1 9inch pie.

Mrs. Leland Shook

# LEMON CHIFFON PIE

| | |
|---|---|
| 1/4 cup cold water | 1/2 cup lemon juice |
| 3 eggs | 2/3 cup sugar |
| 1 teaspoon grated lemon rind | 1/2 teaspoon salt |
| 1 envelope Knox gelatine | |

Soften gelatine in water. Cook beaten egg yolks, sugar,
lemon juice and salt in double boiler until custard
consistency. Add gelatine, rind. Cool. When mixture begins to
thickens add stiffly beaten egg whites to which 5
tablespoons sugar has been added. Turn into baked
pie shell and chill. 1/2 cup cream whipped may be
added for richer pie

Edith Adkins

# MINCE MEAT

3 pounds lean beef, ground coarse
1 pound suet, ground fine
3 pounds seeded raisins
1 gallon juicy apples
1 pound currants
3 pounds brown sugar
½ pound citron
1 tablespoon allspice
1 tablespoon cinnamon
1 tablespoon nutmeg
scant ½ cup salt

Mix above well and add 3 pints cider or hot beef stock. Mix again and add 4 oranges and 1 lemon cut fine. When making pies, add lemon and vanilla (about 1 teaspoon each for 2 pies) and enough fruit juice to make moist, pineapple or grape juice is excellent. Recipe makes about 25 pies, and can be kept in a stone crock.

Mrs. R. Ellis Clark

# PECAN PIE

¾ cup brown sugar
1 cup corn syrup (white)
4 eggs
salt
vanilla
1 cup pecan meats

Mix. Put in lump of butter and bake in uncooked crust in slow oven.

Mary Shield

# PEACH PIE SUPREME

one unbaked pie shell
4 - 6 peaches
½ - ⅔ cup sugar
⅛ teaspoon cinnamon

½ cup sour cream
2 tablespoons flour
½ cup grated
Snappy cheese

Line pyrex pie pan with pastry. Cut peaches in eighths or leave in halves. Arrange in pastry lined pan. Mix the sugar, flour and cinnamon and cream. Pour mixture over the peaches. Sprinkle the cheese over peaches and bake at 425° 40-50 minutes. (Variation - substitute apples for peaches.)

Mrs. Kenneth B. Millett

# OSGOOD PIE

3 eggs
1 cup sugar
½ cup butter
1 cup pecans
1 cup seedless raisins
1 tablespoon vinegar
1 teaspoon vanilla
cinnamon, cloves, nutmeg

Mix all ingredients together, pour in a single pie crust and bake slowly for 1 hour in 300° oven.

Mrs. R. Ellis Clark

## PUMPKIN OR SQUASH PIE

1½ cups strained pumpkin or squash
2 eggs, beaten          1 cup milk
8-10 tablespoons sugar  ¼ cup cream
1 tablespoon melted butter ¼ teaspoon mace
½ teaspoon cinnamon     1 teaspoon ginger
    ⅙ teaspoon salt, or to taste

Mix ingredients and pour into a crust. Bake at 400°, lowering temperature to 375°, until filling is set and slightly brown.

E. H. Nostrand

## RHUBARB PIE

Blend: 1½ cups sugar  3 tablespoons flour
    ½ teaspoon nutmeg  2 tablespoons butter

Add 2 eggs to mixture, beat until smooth and add 3 cups chopped rhubarb. Pour into unbaked pastry shell and top with pastry cut into fancy shapes. Bake in hot oven (450°) for 7 minutes; reduce heat to 325° and bake until filling thickens. (about 30 minutes)

Mrs. Robert Cooper Morris

# WHITE POTATO PIE

2 pounds potatoes, mashed and cool
½ pound butter
1 pound sugar
5 eggs
2½ cups milk
½ cup brandy
nutmeg

Cream butter and sugar thoroughly. Add beaten egg yolks, then add the potatoes. Stir in milk, brandy and nutmeg and finally the beaten egg whites.

Pour into 2 uncooked pie shells and bake in 350° oven for 1 hour.

This is better than sweet potato pie.

Mrs. William T. Hammond

# SWEET POTATO PIE

2 cups cooked sweet potato, put through sieve
1 cup sugar
3 or 4 eggs
1 teaspoonful yeast powder
2 cups milk
2 tablespoonsful butter or margerine
1 teaspoonful lemon extract

Cook enough sweet potatoes to make 2 cups after put through sieve, add butter while hot. Add egg yolks one at a time, beat well, add lemon extract and milk. If not sweet enough to suit taste, add a little more sugar. Have your crust in pie plate and pour in mixture. Cook in a moderate oven until done. You can test this by inserting a knife blade.

Beat whites of egg until stiff, adding 3 tablespoons sugar, ½ teaspoon cream tartar, beating thoroughly. Place on top of pie, bake in slow oven until meringue is brown.

If you do not care for meringue, beat egg whites light and stir into mixture before pouring into the pie crust.

Mrs Douglas Hanks

# SWEET POTATO PIE

| | |
|---|---|
| ¾ c. sugar | 2 cups hot cooked mashed |
| ½ tsp. salt | sweet potatoes |
| 1 tsp. cinnamon | 2 tbs. butter (soft) |
| 1 tsp. ginger | 3 eggs |
| ⅛ tsp. cloves | 1¼ c milk |
| 1 tsp. grated lemon rind | 9 in. unbaked pie shell |

Stir together the sugar, salt, cinnamon, ginger
and cloves. Mix in mashed hot sweet potatoes
and butter thoroughly. Beat in eggs, one at a
time. Add grated lemon rind and milk. Beat to
mix well. Pour into unbaked pie shell. Bake in
hot oven (400°) for 40-50 minutes.

## UNBAKED PIE SHELL

| | |
|---|---|
| 1½ c. sifted flour | ½ c. shortening |
| ½ tsp. salt | 3 tbs. water |

In a bowl, mix flour and salt. With two
knives, cut in shortening until size of peas.
Blend in water with fork and mix until
dough holds together. Roll out on lightly
floured board and put into pie pan.

                          Harriet C. Swaine

# CHOCOLATE PIE

2 squares chocolate
2 cups sugar
½ cup cream or milk
½ cup butter
5 eggs, beaten

Boil together all ingredients except eggs until as thick as honey. Cool slightly and add the well beaten eggs. Cool and bake in crust until set.
Makes 2 small or 1 large pie.

Mrs. Jeremiah Valliant

# BANBURY TARTS

1 cup chopped seeded raisins
1 cup sugar
1 egg, beaten
1 lemon, juice and grated rind

Combine all and bake in small squares of thin short pastry.

Mrs. James Dixon

# Strawberry Tarts

Grease mold or 6 tart shells (3½ inch).
Fill with pastry and chill several hours
before baking.- Cool after baking and
brush sides and bottom of tarts with kirsch

| | |
|---|---|
| 2 eggs separated | salt |
| ½ cup Milk | slivered almonds |
| 6 tablsps. sugar | Strawberries |
| 3 or 4 drops almond extract | Currant Jelly |

Mix egg yolks, sugar, and milk in top of
double boiler and cook over boiling water 5 or 6
minutes until thick. Remove from hot water and
fold in stiffly beaten egg whites (egg whites
beaten with a few grains of salt and almond
extract). As it cools pour into tart shells or
mold and press in gently and close together, ripe
freshly washed and hulled strawberries. Chill.
Pour melted (not boiled) currant jelly flavored
with ½ teaspoon kirsch (about 1 tblsp. of jelly
per tart). Arrange slivered almonds around sides
of pastry.

Mrs. George F. Olds III

# PINEAPPLE  UPSIDE  DOWN  CAKE

⅓ cup butter          1½ cups brown sugar
          2 tablespoons pineapple juice
8 slices pineapple     8 red cherries


Place butter, brown sugar and juice in frying
pan. (a large skillet) Heat slowly and stir
until blended. Add pineapple and cherries in
any pattern desired.


1½ cups flour          1 teaspoon vanilla
3 teaspoons baking powder ¼ teaspoon almond
½ cup sugar            ½ cup milk
2 eggs                 3 tablespoons melted fat


Mix above ingredients and beat 2 minutes.
Pour this batter over arranged pineapple in
pan. Bake 35 minutes in moderate oven. Let
stand for 5 minutes and then carefully turn
out on platter. Serve with whipped cream
if desired.

Mrs. Ernest J. Heinmuller

# STRAWBERRY SHORT CAKE

2 cups flour
3 teaspoons baking powder
1/2 teaspoon salt
2 tablespoons sugar
2 tablespoons butter
4 tablespoons shortening
1 egg
   milk
2 quarts strawberries
1/2 pint whipping cream

Sift flour, add baking powder, salt and sugar. Add butter and shortening and cut in fine. Beat the egg and add enough milk to make 2/3 cup. Add this to the flour mixture to make a soft dough.

Divide dough into two parts and roll each part into a sheet about 8 x 11 inches. Place one on a cookie sheet and spread with butter. Put the other cake on top. Bake in a pre-heated oven (375°).

As soon as you take them from the oven separate the layers. When cool, put half of the strawberries, chopped and slightly sweetened between the layers. Put selected whole berries on the top, and cover lavishly with xxxx sugar and serve with whipped cream.

SERVES 12                   Mrs. D. C. Kirby

# ORANGE CAKE

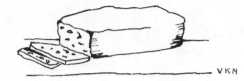

VKN

1 cup of raisins
½ cup English walnuts
rind of one orange.

1 cup of sugar
¼ pound butter or margarine
2 eggs
2 cups flour
1 teaspoon of soda
1 cup sour milk
1 teaspoon orange extract

Cream butter and sugar, add the eggs. Mix well
and then and flour and sour milk alternately,
sifting the soda in with the flour. Grind together the raisins, orange rind and walnuts, and dust
with flour.
Add orange extract, then the nuts, raisins, and
orange peel.
Bake in a moderate oven. When you take it
from the oven, pour on top ½ cup sugar
mixed with the juice of an orange, and
leave the cake in the pan until the sugar
mixture on top crystalizes.

Mrs. Samuel W. Bratt

# POUND CAKE

1 pound flour
1 pound eggs (10)
1 pound sugar
¾ pound butter
1 ounce brandy
1 teaspoon nutmeg
1 teaspoon mace

Cream half the flour with the butter and add brandy and spice. Beat yolks until light – add the sugar and beat well, then the beaten whites and rest of the flour alternately. When this is thoroughly mixed, put all together and beat for a half hour. (With electric mixer, I find 20 minutes is enough.) Bake in tube pan in 300 degree oven for about 1¼ hours.

                    Miss Mary McDaniel

# BANANA AND SPICE CAKE

3 cups flour
½ teaspoon salt
2 teaspoons soda
2½ teaspoons cloves
2½ teaspoons cinnamon
1¼ cups raisins
1¼ cups black walnuts
6 ripe medium size bananas
1 cup butter or margarine
2 cups sugar
4 eggs

Cream shortening and sugar; add whole eggs, one at a time.

In another bowl, mix sifted flour, soda, salt and spices. Then add the raisins and nuts and mix until they are well floured.

Combine the dry ingredients and the sugar and shortening mixture. Add the bananas, each mashed to a pulp.

Bake in a tube pan greased lightly with butter at 350° approximately 1 hour 25 minutes. Test with straw.

Cake improves after being made several days. Can be frozen for indefinite period. Very nice cake for holidays.

Mrs. Earle R. Todd

# RUM CAKE

¼ lb. butter
½ lb. sugar
3 eggs
1 tsp. vanilla

½ lb. flour
2 tsp. baking pwd.
1 cup milk

Cream the butter and sugar  Add eggs, one at a time, beating thoroughly after each addition. Sift flour and baking powder together and add to above mixture alternately with milk to which vanilla has been added. Pour batter into 2 greased cake pans. Bake 20-25 minutes in 350° oven. Fill and frost.

## FILLING

1 lb powdered sugar
1 gill (7 tbs.) rum
3 oz. butter

Cream sugar and butter together; add rum. Spread between cooled cake layers.

## ICING

1 c. granulated sugar
½ c. water
1 egg white
1 tsp. vanilla

Boil sugar and water until stiff enough to string from a spoon. Beat egg white until very stiff and flavor with vanilla. Add to hot sugar mixture and beat until consistency to spread.

Helen Hooper Coble

# CURRANT CAKE

1 pound of currants
1 pound brown sugar
1 pound of flour
4 eggs
pinch salt
1 cup cold water
½ pound butter
1 teaspoon baking powder
1 teaspoon vanilla or lemon ext.

Cream butter and sugar together. Add eggs one at a time, beating thoroughly after each addition. Add cold water. Then flour, mixing well.
Flour the currants and walnuts, if you want. Mix into the batter.
Bake in a moderate oven for 1 hour at 325° and for ¾ of an hour more at 300°.

Mrs. Samuel W. Bratt

# FRUIT CAKE

| | |
|---|---|
| 1 pound brown sugar | ½ pint Brandy |
| 1 pound butter | 1 pound flour |
| 12 eggs | 2 teaspoons baking powder |
| 2 pounds raisins | 1 teaspoon nutmeg |
| 2 pounds currants | 1 tablespoon cloves |
| ½ pound citron | 1 tablespoon allspice |

Sift together flour and baking powder. Cream butter, adding sugar gradually. Beat eggs into this very thoroughly. Sift flour and spices, folding them into batter alternately with the Brandy. Flour raisins, currants, citron and orange peel, and fold them into the batter. Bake in slow oven from 2 to 3 hours.

Mrs. S.N. Hersloff

# WHITE FRUIT CAKE

| | |
|---|---|
| 1 cup butter | 1 cup of milk |
| 2 cups sugar | 3½ cups flour |
| ½ pound conserved cherries | ¾ pound citron |
| whites of 5 eggs | 1 small coconut grated |
| 1 teaspoon baking powder | 1 pound almonds |

Cream the butter and sugar. Add eggs one at a time, beating well after each addition. Sift flour and baking powder, and add alternately with milk. Beat the egg whites and fold into batter. Fold in other ingredients.
Bake for 1½ hours in a moderate oven.

Mrs. Samuel Bratt

# LITTLE QUEEN CAKES

4 eggs, separated
1 cup sugar
½ cup butter
½ lemon

1 cup cake flour
½ teaspoon salt
¼ teaspoon baking
    powder

Cream butter, gradually beat in sugar. Add grated rind and juice of lemon. Beat thoroughly Beat egg yolks until thick, add to sugar mixture. Sift dry ingredients, stir in lightly. Add stiffly beaten egg whites. Bake about 20 minutes in small cup cake tins or paper cups. Bake at 325°.

Mrs. C. E. Partridge

# ONE-TWO-THREE-FOUR CAKE

1 cup butter
2 cups sugar
3 cups flour
4 eggs

1 cup milk
2 teaspoons baking powder
¼ teaspoon salt
2 teaspoons flavoring

Cream butter and sugar. Add beaten egg yolks and beat together. Sift dry ingredients together twice, adding alternately with liquid. Lastly add flavoring. Eggs may be separated, if so add stiffly beaten egg whites last. Bake at (350°) in loaf or layer tins.

Mrs. George Benhoff

# MARBLE CAKE (OLD FASHIONED)

### Light Part:

whites of 7 eggs
1 cup butter
3 cups white sugar
1 cup milk

4 cups flour
½ teaspoon soda
1 teaspoon cream tartar
lemon flavor

### Dark Part:

yolks of 7 eggs
1 cup butter
2 cups brown sugar
1 cup molasses
1 teaspoon each of allspice, cloves and cinnamon

4½ cups flour
1 cup milk
½ teaspoon soda
1 teaspoon cream tartar

Mix each part (light and dark) as a separate cake. When the batters are ready, put into a large round baking pan a spoonful of batter, light and dark alternately, until all batter is used. Bake in slow oven, about 300° until a broom straw inserted comes out dry.

Mrs. C. C. Cooper

Allow all ingredients to come to room temperature. If the ingredients are at room temperature, your cake will be higher and fluffer.

# MAPLE WALNUT CAKE

1¼ cups sugar      ½ cup milk
½ cup butter      2 cups flour
3 eggs      2 teaspoons baking powder

For center of cake or middle layer take
⅓ of batter and add:

1 Tablespoon molasses     1 teaspoon cinnamon
½ teaspoon cloves      1 cup flavored raisins

## MAPLE ICING:

½ block or ½ pound maple sugar
2 cups brown sugar
½ cup butter
1 bottle cream

Cook all together until coats a spoon.
Remove from fire and beat until creamy.
Add walnuts and spread on cake. Add
walnuts to top of cake.

             Mrs. William D. Noble

To prevent icing from running, sift
flour over cake before spreading.

# MATRIMONY CAKE

Part I:
  1½ cups oatmeal flour  (grind rolled oats)
  1½ cups white flour  1 cup butter
  1 cup brown sugar  1 teaspoon baking soda
          pinch salt

Mix the dry ingredients, crumb in the butter with a pastry blender. Take one half of this mixture and pat down in a flat pan. Cover with date mixture, then pat remainder of crumb mixture on top.

Part II:  date mixture
  1 cup brown sugar  1 cup water
  8 ounce package of dates
Boil these ingredients until soft and thick. Cool before putting between crumb mixture above.

Bake in a hot oven for 30 - 35 minutes.

Emily Ewing

# Nut Cake

½ teaspoon grated lemon rind
⅔ cup sugar
¼ teaspoon salt
4 egg yolks
1½ teaspoon vanilla
1½ tablespoons flour
3 cups ground walnut meats
4 egg whites
1 Tablespoon bread crumbs

Add lemon rind to sugar and salt and add gradually to beaten egg yolks and vanilla. Beat thoroughly.

Sprinkle flour over nuts and beat into egg yolk mixture. Fold in stiffly beaten egg whites and pour into a loaf pan (9½" x 4") buttered and sprinkled with bread crumbs.

Bake one hour in a moderate oven (375°)

Ice cake or serve garnished with whipped cream.

Mrs. Francis G. Bartlett

SNT

## CHOCOLATE ÉCLAIR CAKE

| | |
|---|---|
| 6 eggs | 6 tablespoons lukewarm water |
| 2 cups sugar (scant) | 1 tablespoon vinegar |
| 2 cups sifted flour | 1 teaspoon angel food flavoring |

Beat egg yolks, add sugar, beat well; add water and vinegar. Fold in flour which has been sifted 3 times. Fold in well beaten egg whites which have had a pinch of salt added. Add flavoring last. Pour into two large layer pans which have been well greased and floured. Bake at 325° for 25 minutes.

Custard filling : 2 egg yolks beaten, ½ cup sugar, 1 cup milk, 2 teaspoons cornstarch, (dissolved in a little of the milk) 1 tablespoon butter. Mix all ingredients and cook in double boiler until thick. Add flavoring to taste and spread between layers.

Icing for top: 1¼ cup sugar, ½ cup water. Boil sugar and water for 10 minutes or until liquid hairs from spoon. Have 1 egg white beaten to a stiff froth. Pour boiled water and sugar slowly over the egg white, then add 4 ounces of melted chocolate and beat vigorously. Ice top and sides.

Rebecca Jefferson

# Egg Nog Ice Box Cake

1/2 pound butter
1/2 pound confectioner's sugar
5 egg yolks
1 cup chopped almonds
1/4 cup whiskey
   Angel Food Cake
   Macaroons
   Whipped Cream

Put slices of Angel Cake in bottom of spring mold. Cream butter and sugar and add beaten egg yolks. Add chopped almonds and whiskey. Fill mold alternately with Angel Cake slices, egg mixture and crushed macaroons.

Let stand several hours in refrigerator. Remove from mold. Coat sides and garnish top with whipped cream flavored with confectioner's sugar and whiskey. Let stand overnight.

This recipe serves about 16-20 people.

Rum may be used instead of whiskey

Mrs. L. Stuart Lankton

SNT

# Easy Refrigerator Cake

(No cooking. Can be made up the day before)

2 eggs
½ cup sugar
1 square chocolate
1 teaspoon gelatine
3 tablespoons cold water
3 tablespoons boiling water
¼ teaspoon vanilla
Lady fingers or plain cake

Beat egg yolks until thick and lemon-colored. Beat in sugar, add chocolate melted over water, and gelatine soaked in cold water and dissolved in boiling water. Fold in stiffly beaten egg whites. Flavor. Line mold with lady fingers, pour in mixture and chill in refrigerator 24 hours. Or arrange lady fingers and chocolate mixture in layers.

Mrs. Kenneth B. Millett

White sugar should be measured with a light touch, like flour, while brown sugar should be packed down tightly in the cup.

# BOILED FROSTING

2 cups sugar  
2/3 cup water  
2 tablespoons corn syrup  

1½ teaspoons vanilla  
1/8 teaspoon salt  
2 egg whites  

Combine sugar, water and syrup, stir over low heat until sugar is dissolved. Bring to boil, cover saucepan for first few minutes of boiling. Then uncover and boil without stirring until clear and threads from spoon.

Beat egg whites and salt until stiff but not dry. Pour syrup (hot) over egg whites in fine stream, beating steadily. Add vanilla and continue beating until frosting stands in peak. Enough for top and sides of 2-9 inch layers, 3-8 inch layers, or 2 dozen cup cakes.

## BROWN SUGAR FROSTING

Substitute 2 cups firmly packed brown sugar for granulated sugar.

## CHOCOLATE FROSTING

When ready to spread, add 3 ounces chocolate, melted and cooled.

Mrs. Harvey Jarboe

## FLUFFY STRAWBERRY ICING

Add 1 cup crushed strawberries while beating.

Mrs. John G. Shannahan

# CARAMEL ICING

3 cups brown sugar
1 cup cream
1 large pinch baking powder

Put all ingredients in a pan and boil slowly until a firm ball forms in cold water. Remove from flame and beat until consistency to spread easily.

Mrs. D.C. Kirby, Jr.

- - - - - - - - - - - - - - - -

# BEANIE'S BOILED ICING

2 cups sugar
3/4 cup water

2 egg whites

Put sugar and water on the stove and stir together until it begins to boil, but do not stir after it boils. Let it cook until it forms a soft ball in cold water. Pour syrup slowly into the beaten egg whites, beating constantly. Let stand for 10 minutes before spreading.

Miss Julia F. Goldsborough

# COOKIES

# ROCKS

3/4 cup butter
1 cup confectioners sugar
2 eggs, well beaten
1 1/2 cups flour
1 teaspoon cinnamon
1 teaspoon baking soda
dissolved in 1/2 cup hot water

1 teaspoon ground nutmeg
1 teaspoon ground cloves
1 teaspoon allspice
1 pound seeded raisins
1 pound mixed nuts
(black or English walnuts
and pecans best)

Blend together well the butter and sugar. Add eggs. Sift the flour, cinnamon, nutmeg, cloves and allspice. Add half of the flour mixture to eggs and butter. Stir well. Cut raisins in another bowl and flour well. Add these to the mixture, add the nuts. Add soda that has been dissolved in hot water. Stir in the rest of flour and spice mixture. Drop in small drops on tins, bake in a moderate oven, 350°.

Mrs. Mitchell Price

In measuring butter for cakes etc. use what the experts call the water displacement method. Suppose your recipe calls for 2/3 cup fat; then simply fill your measuring cup 1/3 full of cold water, add the fat piece by piece until the water is just at the one cup mark.

## GINGER COOKIES

½ pound lard or butter
¼ pound brown sugar
1 egg
1 orange, juice and rind
¼ teaspoon salt
1 pint molasses
2 tablespoons ginger, powdered
1 tablespoon cinnamon
1 teaspoon cloves
1 teaspoon soda

Heat molasses and shortening. Add soda and cool. Add orange juice and grated orange rind. Stir in flavorings and beaten egg. Add enough flour to thicken. Drop from spoon and bake in a hot oven for 15 minutes.

Kitty Parker Rouse

# CORN FLAKE COOKIES

2 cups brown sugar
2 cups butter or other shortening
2 eggs
3 1/2 cups sifted flour
2 teaspoons baking powder (tartrate)
1 teaspoon soda
1/2 teaspoon salt (or more depending on
                          shortening used)
1 teaspoon vanilla
2 cups cornflakes or krispies

Cream together well the butter and sugar.
Add other ingredients as listed. When dough
is stiff enough to roll in balls the size of a
hickory nut, place in greased pan 1 inch
apart. Mash lightly with a fork and bake
in 350° oven 10 to 12 minutes. Allow to cool
for 1 minute before removing cookies from
tin. Makes about 80 cookies.

Mrs. George T. Olds III


"A farmer always plants 5 grains of corn
        One for the cut-worm
        One for the crow
        One for the black bird
        And two to grow."

# GINGER ANIMALS

3/4 cup butter
1 1/2 cups sugar
2 eggs
3/4 cup molasses

4 teaspoons soda
4 cups flour
1 teaspoon cinnamon
1 teaspoon ginger

Cream shortening, add sugar gradually and cream mixture thoroughly. Add beaten eggs and molasses. Add soda which has been dissolved in about 4 teaspoons of hot water. Sift flour once and measure; sift flour, cinnamon and ginger together and add to first mixture. Chill until firm in refrigerator. Roll on lightly floured board and cut with fancy animal, Santa Claus or ginger cake boy cutters. Bake 15 minutes in 350° oven.

Mrs. Harvey Jarboe

# SANDIES

³/₈ pound margarine
5 tablespoons powdered sugar
1 cup chopped nuts
2 cups flour
½ teaspoon vanilla
1 ice cube

Cream margarine and sugar, flour the nuts. Add flour to creamed mixture, then nuts and vanilla. Allow the ice cube to melt on dough. Mix and form into shape of pecans and bake in moderate oven until light brown and firm. Let cool then shake in a paper bag containing a little powdered sugar.

Mrs. J. Carroll Johnson

\\\ /// \\\ /// \\\ /// \\\ /// \\\ /// \\\ /// \\\ /// \\\

# SPRITZ COOKIES

1 cup butter
⅔ cup sugar
3 egg yolks

2½ cups flour
½ teaspoon lemon flavoring
½ teaspoon vanilla

Cream butter, add sugar, add beaten egg yolks, then flour and flavoring. Put through cookie gun. Bake 8 minutes in 450° oven. Ground nut meats may be added.

Mrs. Harvey Tarbox

### Albany Cakes no. 1

½ lb. butter             1 egg
1 lb. brown sugar        1 cup cream
6 cups flour             1 tsp soda
2½ oz. cinnamon          1 tsp salt

Cream butter, mix sugar and flour,
add salt, cinnamon. To mixture add
beaten egg and cream in which soda
has been dissolved. Roll in granulated
sugar to fairly thin rope like piece.
Roll up as illustrated. Bake at 350°
on greased cookie sheet until brown.

Mrs. P. Kenard Wright

### Albany cakes no. 2

2 eggs                   1½ lb. sugar
1 lb. butter             3 tsp. baking powder
1 cup milk               3 oz. cinnamon

enough flour to make soft dough.
mix ingredients and bake in
moderate oven until brown.

Mrs. Ronald Nevius

328

# FILLED BROWN SUGAR COOKIES

1 ½ cups brown sugar     ½ cup water
½ cup butter            1 teaspoon soda
1 teaspoon vanilla      flour enough to roll out

Mix the above ingredients, adding flour gradually. Roll out and cut. Bake at 375° for 10 to 12 minutes.

When cookies are cool, place 2 together with the following filling:

1 box seeded raisins   ⎫
2 cups sugar           ⎬ boil until thick,
1 cup walnut meats     ⎭ then cool.
1 cup water

Mrs. Charles B. Adams

# CREOLE KISSES

½ pound confectioners sugar
3 egg whites
1 teaspoon vanilla
½ teaspoon cream of tartar
½ cup chopped nuts

Beat the egg whites stiff. Add sugar.
Beat. Add cream of tartar and vanilla.
Fold in nuts and drop by teaspoon
on glazed paper. Bake in a slow oven
at 225°.

Mrs. J. F. Clark

# CHOCOLATE COCOANUT COOKIES

Same as above recipe except double
the vanilla, add ½ cup cocoa and ½
pound of cocoanut.

Nita H. Nevius

"Stir cakes, and do all such things
sun-wise, and never reverse in
making anything, or else you will
undo your work."

# BROWNIES

2 squares of chocolate
1/8 pound butter
1 cup sugar
1/2 cup flour
Pinch of salt
1 egg
1 teaspoon of vanilla
1/2 to 1 cup of chopped nuts

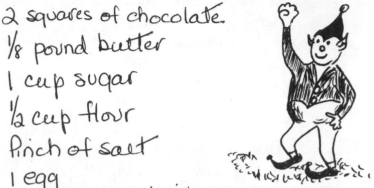

Melt butter and chocolate
in a saucepan — add all
other ingredients and mix
thoroughly.

Bake in greased cake
pan 15 to 20 minutes at
350 degrees.

Mary M. Logan

# Date and Nut Bars

| | |
|---|---|
| 3 eggs | 1/2 teaspoon baking powder |
| 1 cup sugar | 1/8 teaspoon salt |
| 1/2 teaspoon salt | 1 cup chopped nuts |
| 1 cup flour | 1 cup chopped dates |

Beat egg whites and yolks separately. Beat half of sugar into yolks, and fold other half into whites. Combine mixtures, add vanilla and fold in flour, salt and baking powder, which have been sifted together. Fold in dates and nuts. Line a shallow pan (about 8 x 12") with greased wax paper and pour in batter. Bake in 325° oven 20-30 minutes until firm and slightly shrunken from sides. Cut in 4 inch narrow strips. Roll in powdered sugar.

Emily Ewing

# BUTTERSCOTCH ICE BOX COOKIES

1/2 cup butter
1 cup brown sugar
1 egg
1/2 cup chopped nuts
1 teaspoon vanilla

1 1/2 cups flour
1/2 teaspoon salt
1/2 teaspoon baking powder
1/4 teaspoon soda

Cream butter and sugar, add egg. Sift dry ingredients together and add nuts. Combine the two mixtures and add vanilla. Half cup of raisins may be added if desired. Form into rolls in waxed paper, chill in refrigerator over night. Slice thin and bake 8 to 10 minutes in a 450° oven.

If desired nuts may be sprinkled on top instead of mixing in the dough. Or, make a meringue of 1 egg white and 5 tablespoons brown sugar; spread on top of cookies, sprinkle finely chopped nuts over meringue. Bake at 350° until brown.

Variation:
   Or use white sugar, add 3 tablespoons of orange juice and the grated rind of 1 orange.

Mrs. Merton Jarbos

# MACAROONS

1 pound almond paste
1¼ pounds pulverized sugar
whites of 8 eggs
2 ounces of flour

Crumble the paste in a bowl, add the sugar and stir with a wooden potato masher. Then add whites of 2 eggs (not beaten). Stir them in and add 2 more, stir again. Repeat until the eggs are all used and you have a light smooth mass. Then add the flour.

Drop by teaspoonfulls on a baking sheet. Bake in a slow oven. Flour the pans, don't grease them.

Miss Martha Goldsborough

Shredded coconut can be freshened by pouring ½ cup milk over it before using.

# Oatmeal Macaroons

1 cup sugar
1 tablespoon melted shortening
2 eggs
3/4 teaspoon salt
2 1/2 cups rolled oats
2 teaspoons baking powder
1 teaspoon vanilla

Mix sugar and shortening. Add the egg yolks, salt and rolled oats. Add baking powder, beaten egg whites and vanilla. Mix thoroughly. Drop on greased cookie sheets, using about 1/2 teaspoon full to each macaroon, allowing space for spreading. Bake about 10 minutes in a moderate oven.

Mrs. C. Albert Kushele

## OATMEAL SUGAR WAFERS

1 egg                          1/2 teaspoon butter
1/4 teaspoon salt              1/2 cup sugar
3/4 to 1 teaspoon vanilla      1 1/4 cups rolled oats

Beat egg until light, add ingredients in order given and beat thoroughly. Drop from a teaspoon on a greased cookie sheet and flatten down with a spatula. Bake in a slow oven about 20 minutes.

Mrs. Edward T. Bromfield

# OATMEAL COOKIES

1 pound brown sugar
¾ cup butter and shortening mixed
½ cup milk
2 eggs
2 cups sifted flour
1 cup chopped raisins
2 cups oatmeal
½ teaspoon salt
1 teaspoon cinnamon
1 teaspoon soda dissolved in 1 tablespoon boiling water

Mix the sugar and shortening; add the eggs one at a time; add milk; mix in the flour sifted with the salt and cinnamon. Add the oatmeal and the soda.

Drop by teaspoonful onto a cookie sheet and bake in a hot oven. Makes about 50 small cookies.

Mrs. Samuel W. Bratt

# PECAN PUFF BALLS

¼ pound butter
¼ pound pecan meats, ground
1 cup sifted cake flour
2 heaping tablespoons sugar
1 teaspoon vanilla
  confectioners sugar

Cream butter and sugar well. Add flour, nuts and vanilla. Roll into walnut-sized balls, place on greased cookie sheet and bake 20 minutes in a moderate oven. Roll in confectioners sugar.

Mrs. H. T. Furey

---

# BROWN RIM COOKIES

1 cup butter or shortening
1 teaspoon salt
¼ teaspoon if butter is used
1 teaspoon vanilla

⅔ cups sugar
2 eggs well beaten
2½ cups sifted flour

Combine butter or shortening, salt and vanilla. Add sugar, beaten egg and beat thoroughly. Add flour and mix well. Drop from tip of teaspoon on baking sheets, let stand for a few minutes, then flatten cookies by stamping with a glass covered with a damp cloth. Bake in moderate oven (375°) 8 to 10 minutes, or until delicately brown. Makes 4½ dozen.

Mrs. Harvey Jarbos

## PFEFFERNUSSEN
## (BLACK PEPPER COOKIES)

2 eggs                          1 cup brown sugar
½ teaspoon cloves               1 teaspoon cinnamon
¼ teaspoon black pepper         1 cup flour
¼ teaspoon soda                 ¼ teaspoon salt
    1 cup seeded raisins and nuts
    ¼ teaspoon baking powder

Beat egg whites and yolks separately,
then together. Combine ingredients as
in other cookies. Add more flour if
needed — the dough should be stiff.
Drop by tablespoons on greased baking
sheet. Bake in moderate oven about
7 minutes.

                        Donald Korte

# SUGAR COOKIES

2 3/4 cups flour
2 3/4 teaspoons baking powder
1/2 cup shortening
1 cup sugar
1 teaspoon vanilla
1/2 teaspoon salt
2 eggs

Sift baking powder, flour and salt. Cream shortening and sugar, add eggs and beat well. Add vanilla and flour and blend. Roll on floured board and cut. Sprinkle with granulated sugar and bake on ungreased cookie sheet in hot oven 10 to 12 minutes.

Barbara Bromfield

---

# SWEET CARAWAY COOKIES

1/2 cup butter or margarine
2 tablespoons caraway seeds
3/4 cup confectioners sugar
1 1/2 cups sifted flour
1 egg beaten
1 cup nuts, ground
1 teaspoon vanilla

Cream shortening and sugar, add beaten egg and vanilla. Mix seeds and nuts with flour and blend with creamed mixture. Form rolls in waxed paper and chill in refrigerator. Slice and bake in 375° oven 12 to 15 minutes.

Mrs. Johnson M. Fortenbaugh

CANDY

# CRYSTAL PEPPERMINTS

1½ cups sugar
½ cup boiling water
6 drops oil of peppermint

Put the sugar and water in pan, stir until dissolved, and boil until syrup spins a long thread. Add flavoring. Beat until creamy. Drop from the tip of a teaspoon onto wax paper, reheating as mixture becomes too thick. Artificial coloring may be added if desired.

# BUTTERSCOTCH CANDY

| | |
|---|---|
| 1 cup granulated sugar | 1 cup water |
| 1 cup brown sugar | ⅛ cup butter |
| ¼ light corn syrup | 1 teaspoon vanilla |

Combine sugar, syrup and water, and set over direct heat. Stir until sugar is dissolved, then cook without stirring to the stiff ball stage. (A drop in a cup of cold water forms a stiff ball) Add the butter and cook to the hard crack stage for brittle butterscotch. Remove from the fire, add flavoring, and pour into buttered pan. Mark into squares while warm, break into pieces when cold.

Mrs. Thomas M. Carpenter

# CHOCOLATE FUDGE

1 1/2 cups white sugar
1 cup brown sugar
2/3 cup milk
1/2 cake chocolate
1 teaspoon vanilla
butter the size of a walnut

Mix all the ingredients except butter
and vanilla, boil 4 minutes, add
butter and vanilla.

Beat until stiff enough to pour
into buttered pan.

Mrs. Walter McCord

---

# CHEWY CARAMELS

1/2 cake chocolate
2 cups sugar
butter size of walnut

1 cup brown sugar
1 cup corn syrup
1 cup milk

Put ingredients in sauce pan over slow
flame, until disolved.
Boil until it forms a hard ball in water.
Pour into buttered pan and when cool enough
to handle, roll into strips and cut. Wrap in
wax paper.

Mrs. Dale Adkins

# GELATINE DAINTIES

4 tablespoons unflavored gelatine
1 cup cold water
4 cups sugar
1/4 teaspoon salt
1 1/2 cups boiling water
1/2 teaspoon peppermint extract
Red and green vegatable coloring

Heat sugar, salt and boiling water to boiling point. Pour cold water in a bowl, sprinkle gelatine on water, add to hot syrup and stir until dissolved. Boil slowly for 15 minutes. Remove from fire, divide into 2 equal parts. Color one part red and flavor with cinnamon extract. Color other part green, flavor with peppermint extract.

Rinse two pans (8x4) in cold water, pour in candy mixture about 3/4 inch deep. Put in cool place (not refrigerator) allowing candy to thicken for at least 12 hours.

Loosen around the edges of pans with wet sharp knife, turn out on board lightly covered with powdered sugar. Cut into cubes, roll in powdered or fine granulated sugar.

Mrs. Thomas M. Carpenter

PRESERVES

and PICKLES

## PINEAPPLE - APRICOT JAM

1 large can crushed pineapple
2 pounds dried apricots
6 cups sugar

After washing apricots, soak in plenty of water for 24 hours. Crush without draining. Add sugar and pineapple, stir well and bring to boil slowly. Cook until thick (an hour or more) Pack in sterilized jars and seal when cold.

Marie M. Riley

=:==:==:==:==:==:==:==

## GOLDEN CHIPS
### (Preserved Pumpkin)

Remove seeds, pare and slice 6 pounds pumpkin. Cover with 5 pounds sugar and let stand overnight.

Next morning add 3 sliced lemons and cook until clear and thick. Pour into jars and seal.

Mrs. James Dixon

# SUN-COOKED STRAWBERRIES

2 pounds of fruit
2 pounds of sugar

Put ½ cup of hot water in a kettle, add the sugar, and stir until boiling, then add the cleaned and hulled strawberries. Simmer slowly for 5 minutes.

The berries will lose their color and shrink, but take them up and put on a large platter. Cover with glass or netting to keep out insects. Let stand in the sun for 3 days, taking them in at night.

If the sun is extremely hot, move into shade during noon hours. The third day the color will return to the berries and they will plump up and be firm. The syrup will almost jell. Put into jars without re-heating.

Do only two pounds at a time.

(Dark cherries are good this way.)
An old recipe of Mrs. M.T. Goldsborough's of Otwell.

Miss Martha Goldsborough

# GRAPE CONSERVE

2 pounds blue grapes
4 oranges
1 pound english walnuts
1 pound raisins
2½ pounds sugar

Skin grapes. Cook pulp and strain out the seeds. Squeeze oranges; chop nuts; put the raisins, grape skins, strained pulp, nuts, and orange juice with the grated rind of two oranges, also add sugar. Put in a pot and cook until thick over a slow flame. Pack in sterile jars and seal.

Emily Ewing

# STRAWBERRY CONSERVE
## (delicious)

1 quart strawberries
5 cups sugar
Juice of ½ lemon

Boil 10 minutes. Let stand several
hours before putting in jars. Then
stand in sun for several days
until they thicken.

Mrs. Alan G. Day

# PRESERVED DAMSONS

Wash fruit and remove stems. It's
not necessary to pit damsons unless
you prefer to. Use ¾ pound of
granulated sugar to a pound of
fruit — cover with water in a large
kettle. Boil slowly for 3 hours.
Skim off pits as they come to
surface during cooking. Put into
jars and seal. Delicious with
poultry.

Jane S. Offutt

# PRESERVED FIGS

1 pound of sugar for every pound
  of figs

Peel the figs, if you wish, as thin
a peeling as possible. Add sugar in
layers to the figs and let stand
over night. It will make its own
juice.

In the morning boil the figs and
sugar until the fruit is clear. Add
a few slices of lemon if you wish.
Pack in sterilized jars.

Miss Martha Goldsborough

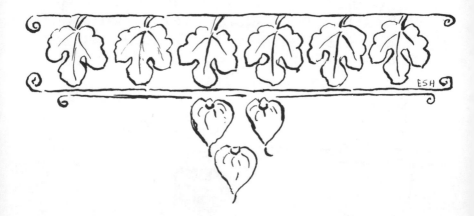

# SPICED PEACHES

5 pounds of whole peeled peaches

2½ pounds sugar

½ cup cider vinegar     1 tablespoon whole cloves

1 tablespoon allspice     1 tablespoon cinnamon

Tie the spices in a bag. Boil the peaches, sugar and vinegar until the peaches are tender. Then remove the fruit and boil juice until thickened. Return the peaches to the juice and allow to cool. Pack in jars and seal.

Mrs. S. N. Hersloff

---

# STRAWBERRY PRESERVE

Cook only two pounds of strawberries at a time. Two pounds of sugar to every two pounds of fruit. Layer the fruit and the sugar in a kettle and bring to a boil. Then cook for 20 minutes. Let stand over night, then pack in jars.

Mrs. S. N. Hersloff

# TOMATO PRESERVES

1 pound yellow tomatoes
1 pound sugar
2 teaspoons ginger
2 lemons, sliced

Wash tomatoes and cover with boiling water. Let stand until skins may be easily removed. (You can remove skins or leave in). Add sugar, cover and let stand overnight. In morning, pour off syrup and boil until quite thick, skim, add tomatoes, ginger, lemons. Cook until tomatoes are clear. Then seal air tight.

Mrs. Woodrow Willey

# BRANDIED PEACHES

Take ripe cling stone peaches, drop them into a solution of soda and water (1 tablespoon soda to a quart of water). Let them stand a few minutes and when you take them out, rub them in a coarse towel to remove down. Rinse in cold water.

Syrup : for each pound of fruit
½ pound white sugar
½ pint water

Boil and skim syrup and put in the peaches. Let it boil 15 minutes. Take out the fruit and pack in sterilized jars. Boil the syrup until it is heavy and set aside to cool.

When cool add 1 pint French Brandy to every pint of syrup. Pour over the fruit and seal.

Miss Martha Goldsborough

# PICKLED CHERRIES

**3 pounds** sour red cherries, pitted
**½ cup** vinegar
**3 pounds** sugar

Place cherries in a crock and pour vinegar over them. Let stand 24 hours.

Drain and add the sugar to the cherries. Stir every day until sugar is completely dissolved.

Pour into pint jars and seal.

These are wonderful served with fowl or meat.

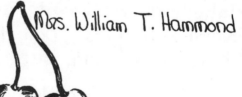

Mrs. William T. Hammond

357

# PEAR JAM

13 pounds Kieffer pears, skinned
10 pounds white sugar
¼ pound green ginger
6 oranges

Grind all the ingredients in a meat grinder and cook until most done. Then add the sugar and cook 20 minutes more.

Pack in sterilized jars and seal.

Miss Martha Goldsborough

# BREAD AND BUTTER PICKLES

30 cucumbers (1 inch in diameter)
10 medium onions
4 tablespoons salt

Slice cucumbers and onions, sprinkle with salt and let stand 1 hour. Drain.

Mix following:
5 cups vinegar, 4 cups sugar, 2 teaspoons celery seed, 2 teaspoons white mustard seed, 2 teaspoons ground ginger, 1 teaspoon tumerie.

Bring to a boil, add cucumbers and onions and again bring to a boil. Simmer 10 minutes. Seal in sterilized jars.

Mrs. Joseph A. Ross

# PEACH AND ORANGE JAM

2 cups peaches, stoned
1½ cups sugar
1 orange

Peel off outer skin of orange, cut in thin strips. Then cut pulp into small pieces. Put peaches and sugar together, chop fine, then bring to boil. Add the orange and rind and cook slowly 40-45 minutes. Pack and seal.

Mrs. C.E. Partridge

# English Chutney

24 ripe tomatoes, cut
4 green peppers, cut fine
12 peaches, cut fine
4 onions, cut fine
½ pound raisins
1 jar preserved ginger in syrup
   or ½ pound candied ginger
4 cups brown sugar
4 tablespoons salt
3 cups vinegar

Cook the above ingredients slowly for three hours or until thick, stirring up from the bottom of the pot. Yields about 7 pints.

            Mrs. Harry Offutt

# PEPPER RELISH

12 red peppers        12 green peppers
12 onions             4 cups sugar
3 tablespoons salt    2 pints vinegar
2 tablespoons celery seed    ½ pint water
        2 tablespoons mustard seed

Grind peppers and onions and scald in boiling water 5 minutes. Strain off water, add all ingredients to peppers and onions and cook 30 minutes. Thicken with a little corn starch, pack and seal. 6 pints.

Mrs. W. S. Seymour

# CRANBERRY RELISH

1 pound (2 cups) cranberries
2 oranges, pulp and rind
⅔ cup sugar (more or less to taste)

Grind berries, orange pulp and rind through chopper. Mix with sugar. Store in jar in refrigerator.

Mrs. Elijah H. Nostrand

# GREEN TOMATO PICKLE

1 peach basket green tomatoes
6 green peppers
6 red peppers
7 pounds sugar
2 quarts vinegar
¼ pound celery seed
¼ pound mustard seed
3 ounces tumeric
¼ pound onions

Slice tomatoes, peppers and onions. Sprinkle with a cup of salt overnight, or for 3 hours at least. Drain in colander, put in kettle with sugar, vinegar and spices and boil until tender.

Pack in sterilized jars and seal.

Mrs. William H. Norris

## PICKLED ONIONS

4 quarts small round onions     1 cup salt
1 quart vinegar     6 tablespoons whole allspice
6 pieces mace     2 tablespoons peppercorn

Peel the onions, cover with cold water, and let stand over night. Drain and cover with a brine made of 1 cup of salt to 1 quart boiling water. Let this stand in a cool place for 24 hours more. Drain and rinse thoroughly.
Heat the other ingredients and when it boils add the onions. Pack after it comes to a boil again.

Mrs. Joseph B. Powell

## CHILE SAUCE

36 ripe tomatoes
8 green peppers    } chop and drain
8 white onions
4 cups vinegar
6 tablespoons salt
3 ounces sugar
2 ounces cinnamon
Allspice, cloves, mace and ginger
   Cook all together 2½ hours

Eleanor Morris

## EUREKA PICKLE

1 peck green tomatoes
3 pounds medium sized onions
6 large sweet peppers
5 small hot red peppers
¾ pint salt
2¼ pounds brown sugar
3 ounces mustard seed
2 ounces celery seed
½ teaspoon black pepper
1 teaspoon tumeric
1 teaspoon dry mustard
3¾ pints vinegar

Slice tomatoes, peppers and onions. Cover
with salt and let stand overnight. Next morning
drain and cover with water. Bring to a boil
and boil slowly for 1 hour. Drain through colen-
der; add vinegar and a little water; return to the
fire and cook slowly 1 hour longer. Last of all
add tumeric and cook 10 minutes more. Take
from fire and add dry mustard.

Yield :   11 to 12 pints

Mrs. John Sowers

# Mustard Pickle

3 cans lima beans
3 cans string beans
1 quart onions
1 dozen cucumber pickles (sweet)
1 gallon green tomatoes (cut small)
2 heads cauliflower
1 dozen red and green sweet peppers

Cover tomatoes, peppers and onions for short time. Cook cauliflower separately.

## Sauce

3 quarts vinegar
1 pint water
5 pounds granulated sugar
2 ounce mustard seed
1 ounce celery seed
3 sticks cinnamon
1 dozen whole cloves
½ cup salt
2 teaspoons tumeric
1 large box colemans mustard
12 tablespoons flour (rounded)

Mrs. E.T. Parsons

# DILL GREEN TOMATOES

Wash and drain firm green tomatoes and pack in quart or gallon jars. To each jar add 1 clove garlic and 2 florets of dill.

Make mixture of 1/3 water to 2/3 malt vinegar, fresh dill, lemon basil, parsley, oregano, marjoram, tarragon and salt. Bring to a boil and pour over tomatoes in jars. Seal and store.

Wye Town Farm

# THE RECTOR'S PICKLES

Use cucumbers fresh from the vine — any size but all uniform. Wash thoroughly and pack in jars.

Mix thoroughly:
- 1 cup salt
- 1 cup sugar
- 1 cup prepared mustard
- 1 gallon vinegar

Cover pickles with the cold brine and seal. Can be used in 2 weeks.

Mrs. Joseph A. Ross

# KOSHER DILL PICKLES

Pack green cucumbers in jars
For each ½ gallon of pickles:
   2 or 3 buttons of garlic
   1 tablespoon dill seed
   ¼ teaspoon alum
   2 or 3 small hot peppers
Pour liquid over pickles while hot
and seal. Keep sealed 90 days before using.

Liquid
   1 gallon water
   1 cup salt
   1 pint apple cider vinegar.

Mrs. Howard F. Kinnamon.

Sweet pickle vinegar should
be saved to use on salads
or in french dressing to
give zest and flavor.

# Spiced Watermelon Pickle

1 1/2 qts. cubed watermelon rind
3 tbsps. salt
3 qts. water
8 cups sugar

2 cups vinegar
2 tbsps. whole cloves
2 tbsps. whole allspice
6 3" sticks cinnamon

Trim off skin and pink flesh and cut rind
into cubes. Soak overnight in the salt and
1 qt. water mixed together. Drain, cover with
fresh water and cook until tender (about 1 hour.)
Drain. Boil together the 2 qts. water, sugar
vinegar and spices which have been tied in
cheesecloth, for 5 minutes. Add the melon
rind and cook until transparent and syrup
thickens, 2 to 3 hours. Remove spice bag.
Pour into hot sterilized jars and seal. Makes
about 3 pints.

Barbara Bromfield

# TABLE OF MEASUREMENTS

## LIQUID MEASURE

3 teaspoons = 1 tablespoon
½ fl. ounce = 1 tablespoon
16 tablespoon = 1 cup
½ cup = 1 gill
4 fl. ounces = 1 gill
4 gills = 1 pint
2 pints = 1 quart
4 quarts = 1 gallon
1 jigger = 1½ ounces
1 pony = ½ jigger

## DRY MEASURE

3 teaspoons = 1 tablespoon
16 tablespoons = 1 cup
2 cups = 1 pint
2 pints = 1 quart
8 quarts = 1 peck
4 pecks = 1 bushel
1 barspoon = ¾ teaspoon

## MISCELLANEOUS

shortening:      2 cups = 1 pound
flour:           4 cups = 1 pound
rice:            2 cups = 1 pound
      1 cup uncooked = 3 cups cooked
coffee: ground  1 pound • 40-50 cups coffee
sugar: granulated: 1 ounce = 2 tablespoons
           2 cups = 1 pound
      confectioners: 3½ cups = 1 pound
      packed brown: 2⅜ cups = 1 pound
cheese: ¼ pound, grated = 1 cup

## SIZE OF CANS

No. 1 = 2 cups          No. 2½ = 3½ cups
No. 2 = 2½ cups          No. 3 = 4 cups
         No. 10 = 13 cups

# QUANTITY COOKING
****

To serve fifty people : : : : : : : :

Chicken salad . . . 5 quarts of cooked
chicken
3 quarts of celery

Mayonnaise . . . . . . . . . . I quart
Macaroni. . . . . . . . . . . 5 pounds
2 quarts medium sauce
Coffee. . . . . . . . I to I¼ pounds
Cream . . . . . . . . . . . . I½ quarts
Sugar . . . . . . . . . . . 100 cubes
Butter. . . . . . . . . . . I pound
spreads 40 sandwiches

Cole Slaw . . . . . . 10 pounds cabbage
Lettuce . . . . . . . . . 5 medium heads
Oysters . . . . . 6 quarts for scallop-
ed oysters
Potatoes. . . . . 12 pounds scalloped
. . . . . 15 pounds for mashed

****

## TURKEY DINNER FOR 160 PEOPLE

8 turkeys averaging 21 pounds each
70 pounds of potatoes to mash
11 pounds of cranberries
18 loaves of bread
24 dozen rolls
6 pounds of onions for stuffing
25 bunches of celery
44 bunches of carrots for shoestrings
44 pounds of string beans
34 cans of kernal corn

****

# INDEX

Apples
   with sweet potatoes, 203
Arroz con pollo, 174
Avocado salad, 233

Bacon
   curing, 125
   sauce, 237
Bananas
   baked in rum, 264
   bread, 48
   cake, 301
   temptation, 264
   with coconut, 265
Barbecue
   beef tenderloin, 134
   chicken, 172
   oysters, 79
   sauce, 129, 172
   spareribs, 130
Beans, ranch, 226

Beef
   barbecued, 134
   chipped, 141, 142
   hash, 136
Biscuits
   Maryland beaten, 34
   orange, 49, 51
   sour milk, 51
   sweet potato, 45
Bisque
   clam, 57
   East Indian, 62
   lemon, 268
   mock crab, 58
   oyster, 55
Borsch, cold, 63
Bouillon, tomato, 70
Bread
   banana, 48
   bran, 32
   cakes, 38
   cheese, 23
   cinnamon toast, 42
   corn cakes, 36
   crackling, 31
   cranberry and orange, 50
   Grandma Scott's yeast, 25

hush puppies, 37
nut, 52
oatmeal, 33
potato, 22
rolls, 24, 26
Sally Lunn, 30
Scotch scones, 32
shredded wheat, 29
southern rice, 48
spoon, 36
steamed pone, 39
Buns, 27, 28

Cake
   applesauce, 304
   banana - spice, 301
   chocolate eclair, 314
   crab, 92, 93
   currant, 305
   double fudge, 316
   eggnog icebox, 317
   fruit, 306, 307, 315
   gum drop, 315
   lemon, 303
   little queen, 309
   maple walnut, 311
   marble, 310
   matrimony, 312
   nut, 313
   one - two - three - four, 309
   orange, 299
   pineapple upside - down, 297
   pound, 300
   Prince of Wales, 308
   refrigerator, 318
   rum, 302
   strawberry shortcake, 298
Candy
   black walnut taffy, 344
   butterscotch, 340
   candied fruit peel, 343
   caramels, 341, 345
   chocolate fudge, 341
   crystal peppermints, 340
   gelatine dainties, 342
   maple pralines, 344
   marshmallow squares, 346
   panocha, 345
   peanut butter fudge, 346

# · · · · MEMORANDA · · · ·

# —·— MEMORANDA —·—

# MEMORANDA

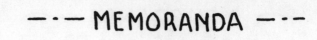

—·— MEMORANDA —·—